ngaji mingan [yawuru]

nyirroogoord minkal [bardi, jawi, mayala]

wayi wanadin [karajarri]

• •

Welcome

Aubrey Tigan Galiwa (dec) preparing a *riji* shell for his last exhibition, 2014.

Sally May, WA Museum MADSC6633/282

AUBREY'S STORY

Talking to old uncle. He said, 'I want a riji'. And he just threw them in the sand, 'This kind riji, this kind, this kind'. Look at them. He had no pencil. He don't believe in pencil. 'This one. This one proper ramu [engraved lines] from Iwany [Sunday Island]. Ramu, that hold everybody in one'. Next day we start with chisel and three-corner file, six-inches nail. It took us 2 to 3 weeks. 'And I want a good one', he say, 'And when you finish it, put on the biidamar properly'. Red ochre got some 'Here uncle' we say. He know how long it took us. He laughed. 'Well, from today on, nobody can't tell you what to do. You clean the shell. You make a riji for use. Then I give them to someone else, to pass him on to his son'. He said, 'It's done and over now. Finished'. Once it's finished you don't talk about it. 'You are a proper aamba'. You know, boss. And you got to be the boss. He'd been the boss for his mob. I've been boss for my mob. And that's how we been. You do your riji, you do your carving, anytime, long as from Saltwater. Nobody can stop you. Boogan liyan waningarra juwar I'm telling you to. That's your Law, your Saltwater Law.

I carve shell for ceremony, for dancing, for our cultural rites. The designs are our history, about the country, about our young people, about old people. If I drop that, we chuck it away, we are lost. You make riji, when you teach anyone, they do that, they keep going you know.

Aubrey and Rosa Tigan (dec) on their last trip to Mayala country in 2011.

Courtesy Sarah Yu

DEDICATION

The exhibition *Lustre: Pearling and Australia* opened in Fremantle, Western Australia, in 2015, following many years of collaboration between the Western Australian Museum, Nyamba Buru Yawuru, and peoples of the West Kimberley to tell extraordinary stories of pearlshell and pearling, for which the region is renowned.

The WA Museum and Nyamba Buru Yawuru dedicate this book to Aubrey Tigan Galiwa, and his wife Rosa, who sadly passed away before *Lustre* opened. A senior Mayala man from the islands of the Buccaneer Archipelago in the north-west, Aubrey was a world-renowned pearlshell carver, passionate about sharing this knowledge and passing it on to the next generation. We trust that *Lustre* honours his life's work and will assist in keeping those traditions alive.

We thank the Yawuru, Karajarri, Bardi, Jawi and Mayala Elders (past and present) and their organisations for their contribution and guidance in producing *Lustre*. We also thank the wider pearling community, past and present, for their generosity in sharing their stories and stories of their families.

We particularly acknowledge those who gave their lives to the industry as divers, skippers, tenders and crew.

Some sources used in this exhibition contain language that today we consider offensive. The Western Australian Museum does not endorse this language of the past and apologises for any distress caused. In addition, please be aware that this publication contains the names, quotes and images of people who are now deceased.

A NOTE ABOUT RIJI

(Carved pearlshell)

The following section contains images of riji. All the items shown are secular in nature; they are not part of the secret-sacred realm. In general, pearlshell art is not held to be secret. However, the objects themselves may, from time to time, be used in ceremonial activities, where they are restricted.

Gaara Riji saltwater pearlshell design engraved by Keifer Yu under instruction from Aubrey Tigan Galiwa (dec).

Courtesy Sarah Yu

FOREWORD

Lustre: Pearling and Australia tells the story of pearlshell and pearling in northern Australia. It brings together the people, the Country, the boats, the shells and the pearls of this historically significant industry in a way that has never been done before.

It explores Aboriginal and Torres Strait Islander Peoples' ancient and enduring relationship with pearlshell, and their participation in an industry built largely on the exploitation of our Country, our men and women, their resources and knowledge, by colonists. It also pays respect to Asian and Aboriginal indentured workers, recognising their contributions and celebrating the cultural exchanges between them — on the sea and in the pearl sheds.

Too many lost their lives at sea.

While labourers were indentured, they lived and worked together. Some of the master pearlers were held in high regard; others were considered little more than slave masters. A culture of support and cultural exchange contributed to a unique human enrichment in this environment.

The elusive beauty of the pearlshell is used to reflect back this story of strength and resilience in the Broome community through their social and cultural interactions. It touches upon the rich social and family histories that come from those encounters. Lifelong relationships were formed and families in Broome to this day are testimony to this love and affection. One of the strengths of this exhibition is how it showcases the unique and diverse multicultural realities of Broome and the power of shared history, born out of the activities of pearling.

Every family in Broome and the Dampier Peninsula is connected to pearling. My own grandfather, Paddy Djiagween, worked on the luggers for a number of the pearling masters, skippering the cargo boat for Dan MacDaniel, sailing fuel and food out to the pearling grounds and bringing back shell.

Importantly, the exhibition is guided by Aboriginal ways of storytelling, ensuring that the Country is ever present and the shell itself holds its own character in the story.

It must not be forgotten that from time immemorial, our Peoples have harvested pearlshell and traded it across the continent as ritual goods of high value. Aboriginal trade of the magnificent *Pinctada* pearlshell had been practised for over 20,000 years before the shell and pearl formed the basis of an industry servicing an introduced economy. The traditions of pearlshell collection and trade are maintained today by Yawuru, Bardi, Jawi, Karajarri, Mayala and Nyul Nyul people.

Courtesy Michel Lawrence, 2016

I wish to express the deep value of this exhibition to the Yawuru people, descendants of the divers and workers with whom we respectfully share the Asian contribution to our social and cultural fabric. Those of us who have been blessed to experience the cultural richness of our community are able to share that experience with others who visit Broome.

The exhibition has been a powerful collaboration between the WA Museum and Nyamba Buru Yawuru, and the beginning of a long relationship.

Lustre reveals the beauty, the hardships, the intrigue, the romance, the greed and the humanity of those who pursued the shell and its elusive treasure.

The elusive treasure of the pearl itself ultimately reflects back to us the elusive treasure pearling has given Broome in creating a continuing culture which values the diversity of the perspectives and experiences of different cultural groups in our community.

Patrick Dodson
WA Senator and Yawuru Elder

AALINGOON

For Kimberley Aboriginal people, their lands and waters — including the pearlshell beds and reef — offer a glimpse of the power and creative energy of Ancestral Beings in the Dreaming.

Aubrey Tigan Galiwa, a renowned Mayala pearlshell carver, tells us of how Aalingoon, the serpent-like being responsible for water and rain, created the pearlshell in Strickland Bay, King Sound.

Full moon rising over the entrance to *Daymango* (The Graveyard), Strickland Bay, King Sound — a traditional area for collecting pearlshell and a place where many hard-hat divers lost their lives.

Courtesy Sarah Yu

AALINGOON STORY

This riji, this is a design of a rainbow snake, Aalinggoon.
Aalinggoon, he came down here into Strickland Bay
from the mainland, down.
He came in to the bay and lives beneath the sea.
He comes out every full moon, when it's a big tide.
As he floats on his back, as he drifts, the scales fall
off his back, and turned into goowarn (guwan) as they
drifted down to the seabed below.
The tides came and chucked them everywhere,
on the reefs, all around the islands.
This way he always gives us more shells.
This is a power.
This is a part of our ceremony.

Aubrey Tigan Galiwa

Aalingoon *riji* by Aubrey Tigan Galiwa (dec).

Courtesy Sarah Yu

MOTHER OF PEARL

Peoples from around the world have, for millennia, shared a sense of mystery and fascination with pearlshell and pearls as objects of desire, wealth, magic and power. Across Asia, Europe, Africa, the Americas and Oceania, mother of pearl has featured as a prestige material — and in many cultures, it continues to do so today.

There are enchanting parallels in the way that pearls and pearlshell, produced by the *Pinctada* (pearl oyster) species, have been understood by different cultures. The shining scales of the serpent-like being Aalingoon are connected with mother of pearl and power. This association between dragons and mother of pearl is not unique to the West Kimberley, it can also be found in a number of Asian mythologies.

The iridescence of mother of pearl is beguiling, but more significant is the commonality of belief in a link between lustre and rainbows, rain, and water, the essence of life.

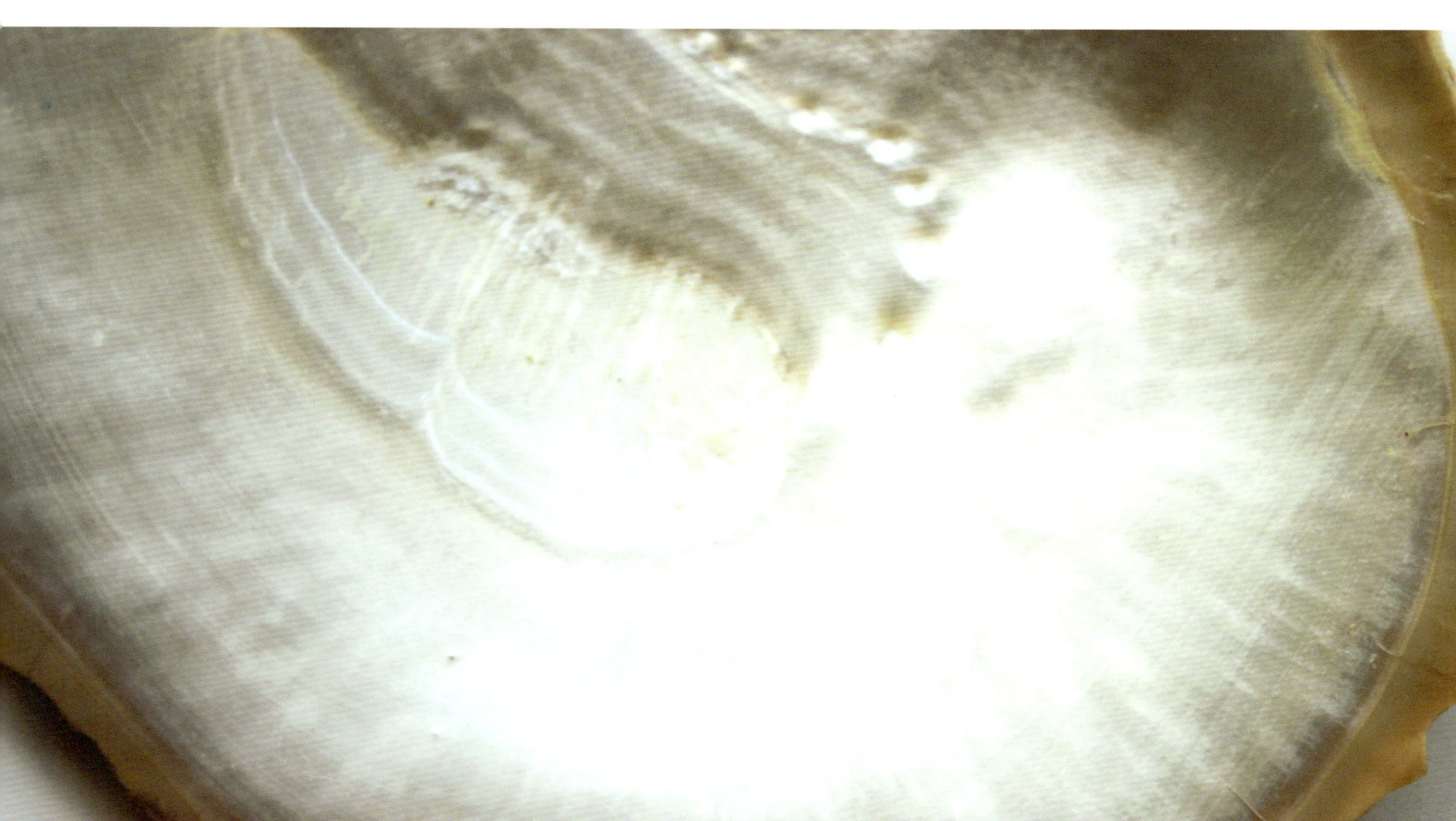

NACRE: AN EVENT OF LIGHT

The iridescent qualities of nacre, or mother of pearl, are not visible when viewed from the side; the surface instead appears dull and flat. Yet when viewed from the top, nacre transforms into a shimmering, reflective surface that seems to radiate rainbow-like light. Iridescence is the result of a dynamic interaction that occurs when light falls on the shell.

Examining a piece of fractured shell under a microscope reveals that nacre consists of platelets made of aragonite — a tough but brittle calcium carbonate also found in substances such as chalk. These layers are separated by even thinner layers of conchiolin, an organic protein, which helps to make nacre uniquely strong, yet flexible and porous. Nacre appears iridescent because the thickness of the aragonite is close to the wavelength of visible light. When light hits the interior surface of the shell, it refracts as it penetrates the surface, and the surface appears to change colour as the angle of view changes.

Scientists are still unlocking the mysteries of nacre and have begun to model artificial bone and hardened glass on the structure of nacre because it combines the qualities of strength, flexibility and porosity.

Left: Scanning electron microscope image of the fractured surface of nacre from *Pinctada* (pearl oyster) showing tablet growth.

Courtesy Prof. Antoni Tomsia, Berkeley Lab's Materials Sciences Division

Opposite: Lustrous mother of pearl.

WA Museum

Above: Aragonite (mineral) platelets are organised like tablets and embedded within the organic matrix (the protein, conchiolin) of a pearl.

Redrawn from Strack (2006) *Pearls*

PEARLING ACROSS TIME AND CULTURE

The social, cultural, spiritual and economic value that humans have placed on pearlshell and pearls can be seen in the stories, songs, imagery, art and artefacts of civilisations, past and present.

OVER 500 MILLION YEARS AGO

Molluscs evolve

Fossil records suggest that a diverse range of molluscan forms were present around 545 million years ago. *Pinctada*, commonly known as pearl oysters, appeared around 13.66 million years ago.

OVER 20,000 YEARS AGO

The ancient value of shell

Aboriginal groups in Australia were some of the first peoples to value the power and beauty of pearlshell. The oldest evidence of this is a 22,000-year-old piece of shell found in a West Kimberley rock shelter. The shell had been carried 200 kilometres from the nearest shoreline.

7,500 YEARS AGO

The first fisheries

The world's oldest archaeological pearl was discovered in a burial site in Umm al-Quwain, United Arab Emirates, and dates back 7,500 years. This is the earliest trace of the ancient pearling tradition in the Persian Gulf, which along with the Gulf of Mannar was home to one of the first pearl fisheries.

This 7,500-year-old pearl was discovered at a Neolithic site in the United Arab Emirates in 2012. The Persian Gulf is historically one of the most prolific sources of pearls.

Courtesy Carl Phillips/Ken Walton

2,500 YEARS AGO

Gems of ancient civilisations

When the Persians conquered Egypt in the sixth century BC, they brought with them pearls, which soon became a fixation of Egyptian royalty. Two hundred years later, Alexander the Great's conquest of the Persian Empire introduced pearls to the Greeks, and later the Romans.

This painting depicts the legend that Cleopatra, in an extravagant display of her wealth to Mark Antony, dissolved a pearl in wine and swallowed it.
Giambattista Tiepolo, *The Banquet of Cleopatra* (1743–44, oil on canvas, 250.3 x 357.0 cm) National Gallery of Victoria, Felton Bequest, 1933

Honolulu Museum of Art. Silk, gilt thread, twill and damask weave, embroidery (detail).
Gift of Mr. and Mrs. William G. Ho, in memory of C.K. and Soo Yong Huang, 1985 (12347.1)

618 TO 907 AD

The mythical pearl

Chinese mythology sees pearls as objects possessing great value and wisdom. The motif of the flaming pearl, chased and revered by a dragon, first appeared in the Tang Dynasty. The pearl's association with serpent-like creatures is paralleled in other mythologies across the world. The Gnostic poem 'Hymn of the Pearl' tells the story of a boy sent to Egypt to retrieve from a serpent the pearl that held the knowledge of the world.

1400s TO 1600s

European exploration

Seeking to satisfy the Spanish Crown's infatuation with pearls, Christopher Columbus found success on his third voyage to the Americas in 1498. Two centuries later, William Dampier became the first European to discover pearlshell beds in Australia.

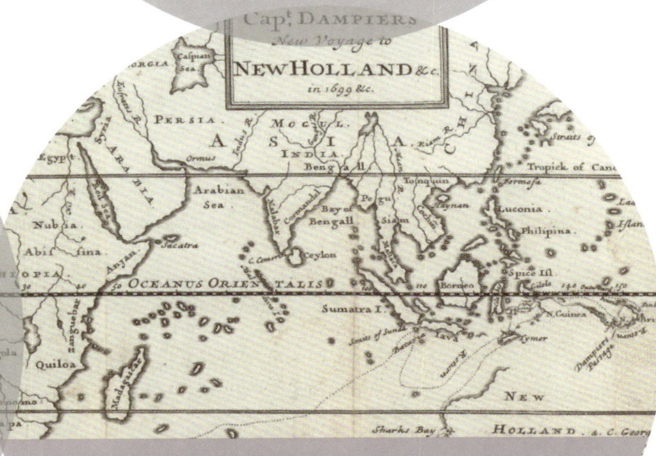

Map used by Dampier during his 1699 voyage, on which he first sighted pearl beds around Shark Bay.
National Library of Australia 1729 MAP NK 11185

1500s

Australian pearlshell crosses the sea

On voyages to northern Australia gathering trepang (sea cucumbers or bêche-de-mer), trochus (sea snails) and turtle, fishermen from Macassar in south Sulawesi also began collecting pearlshell. Aboriginal rock art in the Northern Territory suggests these journeys were occurring as early as the sixteenth century; this represents perhaps the earliest exploitation of Australian pearlshell.

1800s

Etched meanings in shell

Pearlshell had been harvested and prized by Aboriginal people long before European contact, and was traded inland from the coast. Since the mid-1800s *riji* (carved pearlshell) was exchanged extensively between Aboriginal communities across north-west and central Australia. These carved iridescent shells continue to be valued for their associations with water, rain and life.

1850s TO 1860s

An Australian industry is born

The pearl oyster was first collected by entrepreneurs at Shark Bay in 1850, but it was the 1861 discovery of the far larger shells at Nickol Bay that had prospective pearlers flocking to Western Australia. By 1870, Queensland pearlers had established an industry in the Torres Strait.

1880s TO 1914

Broome: 'the pearling capital of the world'

In the 1880s pearlers turned their sights to Roebuck Bay (Broome) in the West Kimberley. By 1910 Broome was the largest pearling centre in the world, benefitting from newly introduced diving suits, fertile waters and a booming international pearl button market. Among the major players were the steadily rising Japanese and Chinese pearlers.

EARLY 1900S

The cultured pearl

The pearling industry witnessed a breakthrough in 1904, when two scientists in Japan, Tatsuhei Mise and Tokichi Nishikawa, patented a technique to cultivate round pearls. They may have accessed the work of Australian scientist, William Saville-Kent, who had already grown half-pearls. In 1916 Japanese pearler Kokichi Mikimoto introduced cultured round pearls to the commercial market.

Mikimoto inserts a nucleus into a pearlshell.

1918

Connections to God

In 1918 the Sacred Heart Church was opened in Beagle Bay. Pearlshell features throughout the church's interior, and mother of pearl adorns the main altar. Mission residents made the 60,000 limestone bricks and helped gather thousands of live shells from tidal reefs. Traditional motifs from the Nyulnyul, Nimanborr and Bardi peoples are included in the designs.

The interior of the Sacred Heart Church, Beagle Bay, decorated with shells, including mother of pearl, cowries, volutes and olives.

Courtesy Sarah Yu

A fleet of custom-built pearling vessels, which replaced the luggers in the 1970s.

Courtesy Paspaley Pearling Company

1950s TO TODAY

Pearl farms: a new era

The pearlshell market waned in the mid-twentieth century after the war and the proliferation of plastic buttons. However, Australia's pearlers gradually forged a new industry of cultured pearl farms, beginning at Kuri Bay in 1956. These farms developed new technologies, safer practices and better understanding of oyster husbandry and sustainability. They continue to innovate today, and remain committed to growing perfect pearls.

THE FUTURE

Continuing a rich history

In 2011 the Australian Government added the West Kimberley to its National Heritage List, in recognition of the significance of the region's pearling heritage to the country's history, culture and indigenous community. West Kimberley coastal Aboriginal groups continue to pass their pearlshell heritage on to their children.

The annual *Shinju Matsuri* (Japanese for 'Festival of the Pearl') in Broome, which celebrates the town's pearling heritage.

Broome Historical Society and Museum 2010-382b

PEARLS AND PEARLSHELL AROUND THE WORLD

Above: *Moka kina*, mounted pearlshell from Baiyer River Valley, Papua New Guinea. Pearlshell *(kina)* was important in *Moka*, complex exchange systems pivotal in establishing and maintaining social relationships.The highly prized shell was scraped, washed, shaped and polished, and often worn around the shoulders of senior men.

WA Museum F1577

Below: Pearlshell ornament.

Courtesy Doug Fong

Above: In the 1930s Bardi Law man Peter Angus Roob gave this *baali-riji* and *binji binji* (hairbelt with engraved pearlshell and pearlshell pendants) to the Wood family at Cape Leveque.

WA Museum MH1950, donated by Aubrey Wood

Left: 'Rising Sun' brooch.

WA Museum CH1970.839, donated by A. Richards

'Happy Days' carved pearlshell, Cossack, WA, c. 1870s.

WA Museum CH1970.459

Butterfly made from pearlshell and turtle shell, West Kimberley, c. 1900s. Many Bardi and Jawi artists made such ornaments for sale, before the use of turtle shell was restricted.

WA Museum MH1943

Pearlshell brooch, north-west Kimberley, WA.

Courtesy Ruth Phelps

Canoe prow ornament, Solomon Islands.
Tied to a canoe's prow at water level this figure was intended to protect the canoe and crew against natural and supernatural elements.
The delicately carved mother of pearl inlay replicates facial decorations.

WA Museum E11774

Carved pearlshell of a dragon, Japan.

Courtesy Kunihiko Kaino and Anna Kaino

PEARLSHELL BUTTONS

In the second half of the 18th century, court fashions dictated lavish buttons for men, and mother of pearl was an ideal material, particularly the white variety. France and England produced the highest quality buttons in the world.

It is not known when the first shell disc was made into a button, but evidence in archives and costume collections suggests a date between 1750 and 1760.

At first, mother of pearl buttons were made by jewellers but, by the last quarter of the 18th century, market demand for shell buttons led to increased mechanisation of the button-making process. There were four steps involved in making a shell button: cutting and smoothing the disc; drilling the holes; inserting the shank; and decorating and finishing the surface. Some shops performed just one step in the process, such as cutting blank discs from a shell. They were then passed along to another shop for the next step. This early form of assembly-line production, in which steps were performed by different individuals on different items, produced infinitely more buttons than a comparable number of jewellers, each working on one button at a time from start to finish.

The mother of pearl from Broome is indeed superb. It is a beautiful nacre. When it comes to the white nacre, Broome comes first. Broome is ahead of all.

Jacky Didelet, Button-maker, Méru (translated by Patrick Amadieu), 2014

Subsequently, as industrial manufacturing processes improved, centres like Birmingham in England and Méru in France began producing large quantities of buttons from shell. These were retailed through jewellers, specialty shops and catalogues.

By the middle of the twentieth century the demand for pearlshell and pearlshell buttons had severely declined in favour of readily and cheaply available plastics. Shifts in fashions, and a great demand for plain, utilitarian plastic buttons during World War Two, also contributed to the demise of the pearlshell button industry.

Today, pearlshell buttons provide a unique record of changing fashions and decorative art styles over time. They also reflect the ideologies, events and interests of their time.

From the 18th century, buttons were produced in Méru, north of Paris — initially as a cottage industry and then in factories. This factory closed in 1955, but was re-opened in 1999 as the *Musée de la Nacre et de la Tabletterie*.

Eric Van Ees Beeck, courtesy *Musée de la Nacre et de la Tabletterie*

When you're walking down the road, especially as it's getting a bit dark, they glitter and they're shiny so that people can see you easily so you can raise bees and honey, which is money, to raise for charity ... When you're born into it, you're proud of it, and that pride takes you to your death.

George Major,
Pearly King of Peckham, 2015

'Pearly King of Dulwich' suit.

Horniman Museum and Gardens
2012.11.1-41

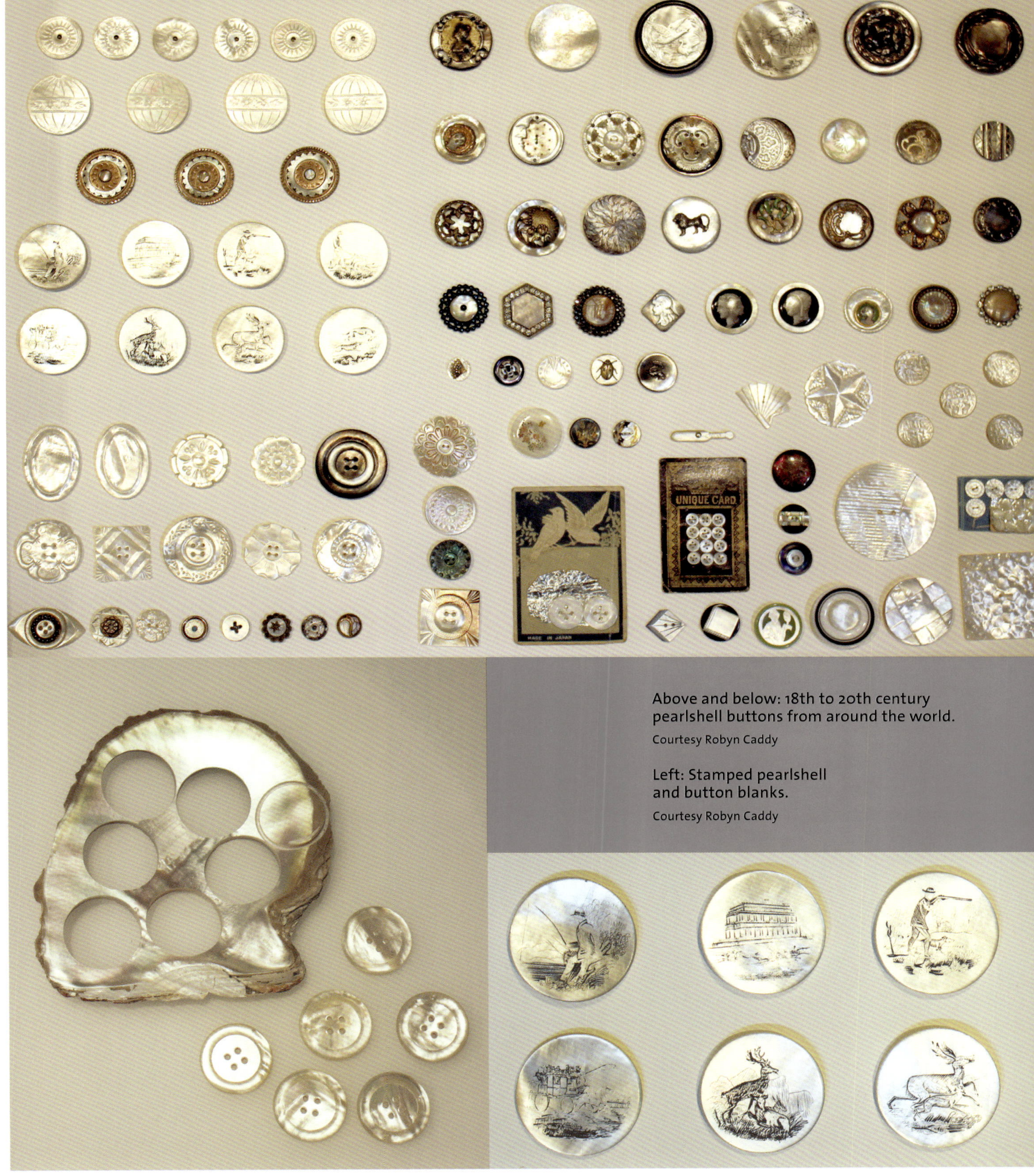

Above and below: 18th to 20th century pearlshell buttons from around the world.
Courtesy Robyn Caddy

Left: Stamped pearlshell and button blanks.
Courtesy Robyn Caddy

PINCTADA

Pinctada (pearl oyster) species are bivalves of great beauty and great age. These shells, with their captivating mother of pearl interiors, belong to the most diverse marine phylum on the planet, the mollusca. Mollusca have an ancient fossil record dating back almost 550 million years. They include well-known groups such as gastropods (snails), cephalopods (octopus), scaphopods (tusk shells) and other bivalves (clams, edible oysters and mussels). While other bivalves such as giant clams can produce pearls, the absence of nacre producing cells means these pearls are smooth, hard, opaque nodules made of the same white calcareous material as the shell. Only species that produce nacre as part of their shell can produce beautifully lustrous pearls.

Courtesy Paspaley Pearling Company

THE PINCTADA FAMILY

Australia is home to nine species of *Pinctada*. Of these, only four are harvested commercially in the tropical coastal waters of northern Australia: *Pinctada maxima, Pinctada albina, Pinctada imbricata fucata* and *Pinctada margaritifera.*

Pinctada maxima is one of the most coveted species because of its enormous shell and very white and thick nacre. It is renowned for producing some of the largest and most lustrous pearls in the world. Today, the famous *Pinctada maxima* pearls are known and marketed as South Sea Pearls.

PINCTADA MAXIMA

Pinctada maxima is the largest, and one of the most abundant and attractive mother of pearl shells in the world. In the wild, shells can live up to 20 years and the largest known shell, found in the Torres Strait, measured 250 mm x 282 mm. The colour of the nacre (mother of pearl) determines the colour of the pearl and there are two different colour varieties: the white or silver-lipped oyster which produces white coloured pearls and the gold-lipped oyster which produces gold coloured pearls.

PINCTADA MARGARITIFERA

Pinctada margaritifera produces a black pearl and has a rich bronze-toned nacreous interior edged with greyish black. The species is found in commercial quantities in the more southerly areas of the Pilbara coast, Western Australia. In French Polynesia, the Cook Islands, Okinawa and other South Sea islands this species is farmed for its black pearls.

PINCTADA IMBRICATA FUCATA

Pinctada imbricata fucata or the Akoya pearl oyster is extensively farmed in Japan for its smaller pearls, known for their neutral tones and fine lustre.

Images WA Museum

PINCTADA ALBINA

Pinctada albina is found in commercial quantities in Shark Bay, where it was harvested mainly for its small, natural pearls. Further north, it is one of the most popular shells harvested by coastal Aboriginal groups, where it is called *li*.

CREATING PEARLS

Pearls can form as a result of an oyster's own nacre-producing cells growing abnormally or as a result of foreign material such as shell, small stones, grains of sand or even parasites entering the pearl oyster. These occurrences initiate a cascade of events, triggering pearl formation as a response. The oyster encases the 'object' in a pocket of mantle tissue known as a pearl sac. Once the pearl sac has formed, external shell is deposited first, followed by internal shell (nacre). This is why pearls are described as 'inside out' shells. Over time, layer upon layer builds up to form the nacreous deposits we call a pearl.

Typically a pearl oyster will reach its adult size within 2–3 years, and it will tend to grow during the warmer summer months. The thickness of nacre in pearl oysters is influenced by the smallest changes in water temperature, and may vary considerably according to season.

Juvenile *Pinctada maxima* under the microscope 21 days after spawning.
Courtesy Cygnet Bay Pearls

PEARLSHELL COUNTRY

The pearling beds around Broome are a natural phenomenon, literally millions of huge pearlshell scattered across the ocean floor, the likes of which not found anywhere else on earth. They are nurtured by a unique marine environment perfectly suited to them, creating a population of extraordinary abundance, concentration and size, one of the great natural wonders of this world.

James Brown, Pearl Farmer and Marine Biologist, 2017

Pearl oysters are found in the waters of several countries bordering the Indian and Pacific Oceans and some countries along the Eastern Atlantic Ocean. Many of these countries, particularly those in Asia, are interested in pearl oyster farming and pearl culture. The warm tropical and sub-tropical waters of northern Australia are famous for *Pinctada maxima*, and the strong currents and tides bring tiny particles of 'food' to the shell, which are sorted on the surface of their gills.

Above

Sunday Island at lowtide,
Kimberley, WA.

Kim Akerman, WA Museum DA-KA1226

Encrusted *Pinctada maxima* pearlshell in a garden bottom of sponges, corals and bedrock.

Clay Bryce, WA Museum

Diving, it's a paradise. I've never seen anything like it down the bottom of the sea. Where there's hundred fathom, pearlshell, coral. Beautiful. It's paradise.

Roy Wiggan Bagayi, Bardi Elder (dec), 2015

When pearl divers look for a good place to find pearlshell they look for seabed that has 'bottom', of which there are various kinds — 'potato', 'garden', 'collar', 'asparagus', or 'whip' which are distinguishable by the dominant species that surrounds the pearlshell oysters. These seabeds are mostly flat, often covered by fine sediments that obscure the underlying rock surface, and are set between areas of mud and sand.The shells become encrusted with other marine life and buried in the sediments, making the shell camouflaged and hard to see. Juvenile oysters develop byssal threads, which are exceptionally strong, silky fibers that are sticky and secure an animal to a substrate. This can assist the animal in staying secure, important in rough seas during cyclones, which occur seasonally along the northwest coast.

... the big tides bring a rich soup of organic particles to the oyster ... but the tides don't just wash in and out of the shells, the oyster feeds itself, constantly beating the water through with tiny hairs on its gills ...

Dr Lindsay Joll, WA Marine Research Laboratories, 1991

Pinctada maxima oyster populations are relatively spread out and not as clustered or gregarious, like other oysters and mussels. Divers call the areas where the shell congregates 'patches', and these areas are named and mapped.

The pearling beds off Eighty Mile Beach, in north-west Australia, are unique in the world because of the vast amounts of shell found there. Over the years populations have demonstrated their remarkable ability to regenerate in the face of often heavy exploitation by pearlers. Today these pearlshell beds are relatively pristine, untouched by pollution, and are protected from over-exploitation by a strict governmental quota system, and the formation of new coastal marine parks.

Pearling bed charts, Buccaneer Archipelago to Bedout Island, c. 1910.

Broome Historical Society and Museum 2013-216. Courtesy Michael Torres Jalaru

GUWAN

We are true Salt Water people. We live off the sea. When I make riji (engraved pearlshell) I think of everything out in the ocean — the loo (currents), the spout, the waves, the land and under the water. All got their own spirit.

Aubrey Tigan Galiwa, Mayala Elder (dec), 2012

Bardi dancer Moochoo Frank Davey Jr.

Courtesy Jordan Shields

Roy Wiggan Bagayi (dec) with his dog on *galwa* (Bardi raft) near *Iwany* (Sunday Island), WA, 1998.

Patricia Vinnicombe, WA Museum DA-PV-2009-08-255

Some of the first people to appreciate the power and beauty of pearlshell were the coastal Aboriginal groups of the north-west Kimberley coast. Collecting the shell on the king (highest) tides, these people have shaped and engraved pearlshell to celebrate country and traditions. People continue to value both *guwan* (undecorated shell) and *riji* (engraved shell) in dance and ceremony, and as important items of exchange.

A LONG WAY FROM THE SEA

With its lustre hidden by carbonate crust, a tiny piece of nacreous shell found 75 centimetres below the surface in a West Kimberley rockshelter is the oldest Australian evidence that pearlshell has traditionally been greatly valued by Aboriginal people. The shell was left at Widgingarri Rockshelter 22,000 years ago. Today, Widgingarri sits on the coast, but 22,000 years ago, when sea levels were much lower, this site was over 200 kilometres from the sea.

Even earlier, Aboriginal people carried other types of shell over great distances. Examples of shell movement include 32,000-year-old baler shell from Widgingarri, 32,000-year-old cone shell beads from Mandu Mandu Creek, 30,000-year-old tusk shell beads from Riwi, and 24,000-year-old baler shell from Shark Bay. The Riwi beads, found 500 kilometres from the ancient coast, are an exciting glimpse of an early long-distance network.

Today, cultural materials such as *guwan* and *riji* are prized items in Aboriginal exchange networks across much of Australia. Far from the shore but still connected with water, pearlshell is a vital element in Central Desert rainmaking ceremonies.

Sarah Ah Choo (dec) preparing *barrgayi* (tusk shell beads) for boys who are approaching initiation in the West Kimberley, 1974. More robust than pearlshell, such beads were also valuable items of trade for the women who made them.

Kim Akerman, WA Museum DA-KA566

Audaby Jack (dec), Bardi Elder, 1981.

Moya Smith, WA Museum DA-MS1981

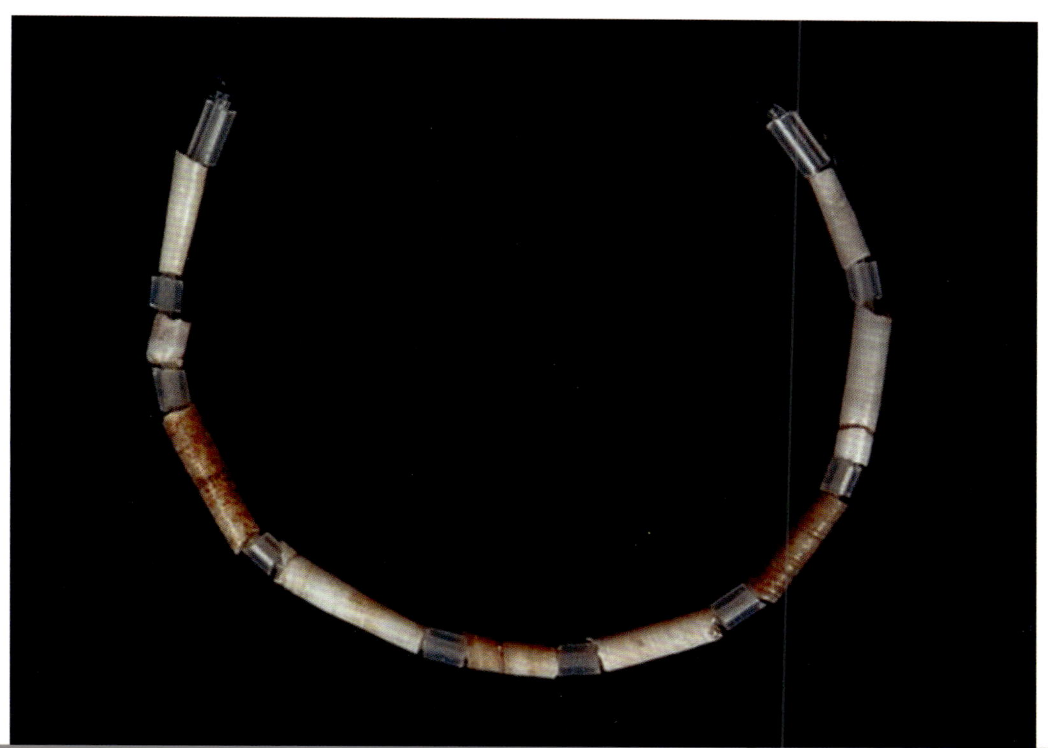

30,000-year-old dentalium beads from Riwi rockshelter.

Courtesy Mimbi Community

They send 'em away ... shield, spear, belt, boomerang, red ochre, paint, shell, everything ... When they get together, they make 'em part of the family.

John Dudu Nanggariny, Karajarri Elder, 1997

Below: Bardi and Jawi men on *Jayirri* (*Tyri/* Jackson Island) in King Sound, WA, 1917.

William Jackson, North West Scientific Expedition. WA Museum DA9312-162

ANCIENT TRADE

For at least 30,000 years Aboriginal people have carried baler shell, pearlshell and tusk and cone shell beads extraordinary distances from the coast. The complex exchange networks that Yawuru and Karajarri, Bardi and Jawi, and Worrora people have traditionally engaged in are known as *yinyali*, *anyja* or *wunan* in their respective languages. Prized items at the centre of these networks, such as pearlshell, weapons and personal gifts, are key in Indigenous rituals, mythology and social relationships.

Exchanges were made through chains of partners on either small-scale (interpersonal) or large-scale (inter-group) levels. As items moved further away from their source, following well-known pathways, songlines and Dreaming tracks — and, later, modern roads, station tracks and flight paths — their meanings often transformed.

It is not known precisely when these networks began, but the movement of specific types of stone tools, hints of shared words in different languages separated by vast distances, and the Dreaming stories told by people, all suggest that they were in place well before the arrival of Europeans.

People might come from the east to our country. Old people will give them something ... give them gifts with little carvings to take back to their home where they never see anything like that.

Lulga Francis Djiagween, Yawuru Elder, 2015

Trade items including pearlshell, spears and shields set out for exchange.

Kim Akerman, WA Museum DA-KA248

Distribution and movement of Kimberley pearlshell.

Map redrawn from original as published in Akerman and Stanton (1994) *Riji and Jakuli: Kimberley Pearlshell in Aboriginal Australia*

One of the things about the Kimberley pearlshell, particularly the engraved shell, because they are so distinctive, they were used by a number of people to start to actually construct maps of some of these ancient trade routes.

These networks went across the continent. Pearlshell probably covered more than two thirds of Australia, Kimberley pearlshell.

Kim Akerman, Anthropologist, 2013

FROM GUWAN TO RIJI

While neighbouring people along the Kimberley and Pilbara coasts made engravings and paintings on rock outcrops and rockshelter walls, pearlshell became the 'canvas' for the coastal peoples of the region stretching from Eighty Mile Beach to Dampierland.

To the Saltwater people of Australia's north-west, the brilliance and shimmer of *guwan* (undecorated pearlshell), is considered to be water, the sea and life itself.

Saltwater people clean and shape *guwan*, and incise *ramu* (lines) onto it to create designs. Natural ochres are rubbed into the *ramu* to make *riji* (decorated shell) that tell cultural and historical stories. Smaller carved blades of shell, *binji binji*, are worn as headpieces, or as shell clusters attached to *baali* (hairbelts) and armbands. Some have gender restricted, esoteric meanings and are powerful ritual objects.

The act of carving and of wearing or holding *riji*, is a powerful boost to an individual's *liyan* — physical, emotional and spiritual well-being — and expresses connection to country and ancestors. Families are extremely proud when they see young men first appear wearing the *riji*. They are given these *riji* in ceremonies to mark their transition to adulthood. Every time people produce or wear *riji, binji binji* or *barrgayi* (tusk shell necklaces) they celebrate culture and belonging to Saltwater Country.

Above

Barrgayi and *binji binji*, dentalium shell necklace, Broome, WA, 1912.

WA Museum E5241

Below

'Warriors of Roebuck Bay'. Naturalist William Saville-Kent photographed a group of Yawuru men dressed for ceremony on Kennedy Hill, Broome, WA, c. 1884.

William Saville-Kent (1897) *The Naturalist in Australia*

Left: Hair belt with carved pearlshell, Roebuck Bay, WA, c. 1890s.

South Australian Museum A3989

Above: Undecorated pearlshell pendant with *binji binji* on hairbelt, Lombadina Mission, West Kimberley, WA. Collected by Reverend Father Nicholas Emo, 1915.

WA Museum E6220

When the boys dance, the binji binji tinkle like keys and the sound makes the women cry because they are so proud of their sons. They can get married now.

Roy Wiggan Bagayi (dec), Bardi Elder, 2010

Possum fur and hair belt with *riji* pearlshell, Roebuck Bay, WA, c. 1890s.

South Australian Museum A3987

CELEBRATING COUNTRY AND CULTURE

While many early pearlshell artists remain unknown others, such as Biggie Albert, Jack Wherra, Butcher Joe Nangan, Bonny Angus, Sandy Paddy Malilboor and Aubrey Tigan Galiwa, have gained international reputations. These *riji* carvers were deeply linked with their ancestors, their culture and their country. Their work includes stories or designs from the spirits of their homeland, the animals, plants and marine life, and historical events such as the arrival of the pearling fleets.

Inspired and taught by their Elders, young pearlshell artists continue to carve new and old stories, creating their own cultural interpretations.

When I carve pearlshell with the old designs I feel good and strong, connected to my father, my grandfather, my country. They come to me in dreams and tell me what to do, and what to carve. That's my inspiration.

Aubrey Tigan Galiwa, Mayala Elder (dec), 2011

Bardi cultural dancers performing at the *Lustre: Pearling & Australia* opening in Fremantle, 2015.

WA Museum

Above: Butcher Joe Nangan (dec) carving pearlshell, Broome, WA, 1981.

Kim Akerman, WA Museum DA-KA4221

Below right: Bardi Elder Sandy Paddy Malilboor (dec) working with red ochre, Lombadina, WA, 1988.

Moya Smith, WA Museum DA-MS1988-08-05

Right: 'Story shell' by Butcher Joe Nangan (dec), is an Aboriginal depiction of the arrival of pearlers.

Broome Historical Society and Museum 2002-823

Below left: 'Cod Is Love', carved shell, Sunday Island, WA, 1927.

Macleay Museum, University of Sydney ETA2014

FINDING SHELL

Stand back you shallow water man,
Let a deep sea diver through.

Saltwater Cowboy, lyrics by The Pigram Brothers, 1997

The tender hoists his diver's bag loaded with pearlshell onto the lugger, c. 1920s.

Bourne Collection, WA Museum MHL 367

Pearlshell oysters lie at the bottom of the ocean. Men and women have risked their lives to find them and the 'jewels' that may lie within.

From traditional shell gathering to modern hookah diving, methods of collecting pearlshell have changed as the industry progressed. For a long time mother of pearl was in demand for manufacturing buttons, but when plastic replaced shell, pearlers turned to cultured pearl farming, focusing on the pearls themselves.

Staged image of a Torres Strait Islander hard-hat diver collecting shell.

Frank Hurley, National Library of Australia 4851320

PEARLING BEGINS

Long before European exploration of northern Australia, fishermen from the Indonesian archipelago visited the coastline seeking trepang (sea cucumbers) and trochus (sea snails). They traded cloth, knives, food and tobacco with local people in exchange for access to fishing areas.

In 1699, English explorer William Dampier noticed pearlshell oysters in the waters off Shark Bay. Over a century later surveyors and pastoralists confirmed his findings. An industry developed, driven by demand for mother of pearl, which transformed the north of Australia from Shark Bay to the Torres Strait.

The foundation of the early industry depended upon Aboriginal and Asian crews, often forced into service, who dived in the dangerous coastal waters, going deeper and deeper in their search for mother of pearl.

A group of Aboriginal women cleaning and drying trepang for export. Photographed by pearler Reg Bourne, c. 1920s.

Bourne Collection, WA Museum MHL 787

Above

Enduring signs of the presence of pearlers and their activities may be seen in the rock art of coastal groups. This image of a steamship, possibly depicting pearler Charles Broadhurst's SS *Xantho*, is from Ngarluma Yindjibarndi country.

Courtesy Alistair Paterson

Right

Pearlers initially collected the small *Pinctada albina* in Shark Bay, but by the 1860s had progressed to harvesting larger *Pinctada maxima* off the Pilbara coast and in the 1880s off the Kimberley coast. Photo of Kimberley pearlshell being opened, c. 1920s.

WA Museum MHL 394

POGEY POTS IN SHARK BAY

Commercial pearlers first came to Malgana country at Shark Bay in 1850, after government surveyor Lieutenant Benjamin Helpman discovered *Pinctada albina* oyster shell there. His first attempt to collect shell at Shark Bay resulted in a take of 3,000 shell pairs.

The industry that developed over the next few decades was unique to north-western Australia, with a focus on tiny seed pearls. Pearlers collected the shell simply by dredging (raking) the shell beds in shallow waters. Similar to the emerging pastoral industry, Shark Bay pearling depended on Aboriginal people's labour. This included boiling rotting shell meat in pogey pots to release the valuable pearls — a very smelly process.

The presence of *Pinctada albina* in such shallow waters facilitated an efficient and easy method of shell collection for pearlers who made their own dredges and rakes. However, by the 1870s, the explorer and infamous blackbirder Captain Francis Cadell and other pearlers such as Charles Broadhurst were using small wooden boats and dredgers to trawl for shell in deeper waters. They set up camps in traditional 'shell places' such as *Wilyah Miah* in Shark Bay.

European pearlers were joined by Chinese entrepreneurs, who worked hard and lived frugally, eventually outnumbering the Europeans three to one.

In 1886, the Europeans petitioned to have the Chinese excluded from Shark Bay and the Colonial Government introduced restrictions on seabed leases. In the face of growing racism, and as a result of the restrictions, Chinese pearlers lost their livelihoods. They were effectively forced to sell their equipment and leave the industry and the area.

Having dredged the seabeds bare at Shark Bay, pearlers moved north, where an industry focused on the *Pinctada maxima* shell was beginning to thrive. They left behind a legacy of places such as the sleepy fishing hamlet of Denham, with its roads fashioned by crushed pearlshell. Aboriginal artists continue to collect shell for carving to this day.

In my time, the pearl boy used to come in from Broome and buy the pearls, and when the war finished, the pearlshell industry closed up in Denham.

Jimmy Poland (dec), Malgana artist, 2012

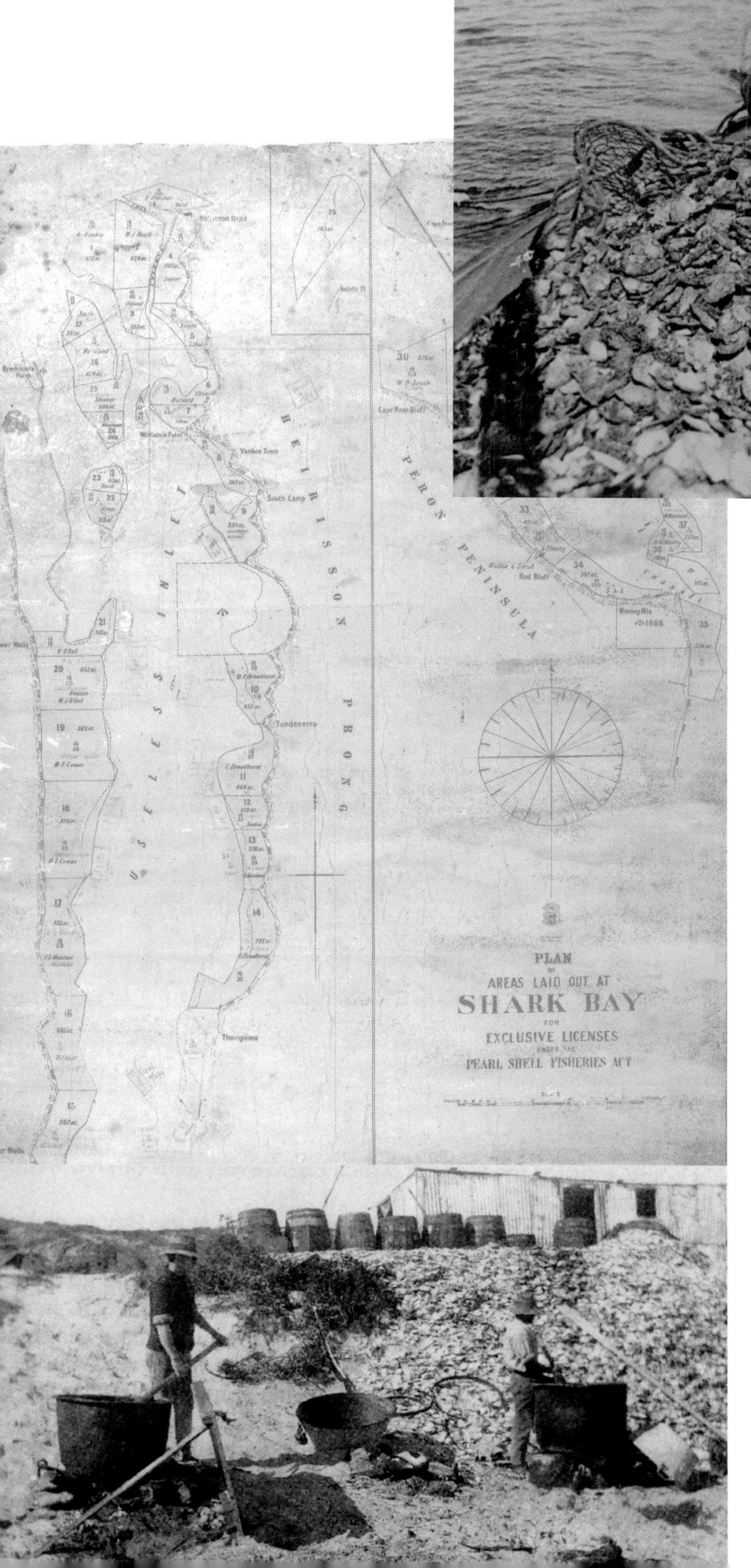

Left

Plan of the areas laid out at Shark Bay for Exclusive Licenses, showing the 'fencing' of the pearlshell beds under the *Pearl Shell Fishery Act 1886*.

WA Museum MHA 4570/001

Above

Shark Bay pearlers Mick and Jack Fry returning with a day's haul of *Pinctada albina* pearlshell.

Dick Hoult, WA Museum MHD 401/026

Below

Boiling the shell in pogey pots.

Courtesy Hugh Edwards (1999) *Shark Bay through four centuries 1616 to 2000*

Opposite

Artwork by Jimmy Poland (dec), ex-pearling worker and Aboriginal artist from *Gutharraguda* (Shark Bay).

Helena Bogucki, Denham studio notes with Jimmy Poland, courtesy FORM

DRY SHELLING

The discovery of the larger *Pinctada maxima* shell in Nickol Bay and the West Kimberley in the 1860s saw commercial pearling begin in earnest. In 1866, struggling pastoralist W.F. Tays asked his pearlshell-adorned Aboriginal servants to reveal their 'shell places'. Newspaper reports of his success finding bountiful pearlshell beds spread through the colonies. The race to collect shell began: shepherds abandoned flocks, sailors deserted and even prosperous settlers became pearlers overnight.

With no roads or ports in Australia's north-west, transportation was a problem. Yet within months of Tays' find, motley towns such as Cossack grew as traders of all nationalities set up shop, building timber boats and erecting makeshift jetties.

Pearlers relied on local Aboriginal people, who showed them where the pearlshell beds were and collected the shell by dry shelling, or beachcombing. Paid only with rations, the local Ngarluma people from stations near Nickol Bay adapted their traditional skills, collecting the plentiful shell by hand on low spring tides for their bosses. For many pastoralists, dry shelling provided a much needed additional income.

The shallow beds were soon depleted and labour became scarce. Larger operators working from bigger boats in deeper waters required divers, so pearlers spread further north in search of Aboriginal labour, or to Malaysia to indenture labour.

Dry shelling by smaller operators continued through the pearling boom and the practice was maintained by several Aboriginal groups of the north-west. In 1968, when the Conciliation and Arbitration Commission ruled for equal wages amongst Aboriginal and non-Aboriginal workers in the cattle industry, many station owners refused to pay wages and Aboriginal labourers were forced to leave. For the Ngarla people, traditional shell places such as *Jijila*, at the mouth of the De Grey River, provided an important source of income for those no longer working in the pastoral industry.

We used to follow the tide, walking for miles, picking up shell all round Yalanban [Thangoo], where our people lived. You would just see the shape in the sand. They were everywhere.

Lulga Francis Djiagween, Yawuru Elder, 2015

Above

Wompa cleaning shell at *Jijila*, traditional pearlshelling camp near Condon, WA, c. 1960, after his group's tin mining venture failed with the drop in price of tin.

Courtesy John Wilson

Below

Beachcombers and dry shellers collected pearlshell from reefs such as these near Onslow, WA.

Arthur Collett, WA Museum MHD 313/32

FREE DIVING

Free diving, or swim diving, gave pearlers access to pearlshell in deeper waters. In the Torres Strait, where Captain William Banner initiated pearling in 1869, local Aboriginal divers were used to collect shell for pearling masters. Finding shell was difficult in the murky, nutrient-rich tidal waters. Often the only way to find the encrusted shell was to spot the glint of the black, white or orange mantle of a gaping shell.

Soon after Captain Banner's success in Torres Strait, other successful pearlers, such as James Clark and Co. brought their fleets containing experienced divers to work the pearling grounds in the north-west.

In north-western Australia, Aboriginal men and women were rounded up because their sharp eyesight and water skills made them highly sought after divers. Diving feet first into the water, they were required to bring back at least ten pairs of shell per day. The work was hard, monotonous and sometimes deadly.

In these remote places, there was little government protection. Some pearlers were considered 'good masters', while others — such as the McRae brothers, who operated the *Dawn* — had a bad reputation. Brutality and ill treatment were commonplace and Aboriginal people recorded their stories in songs that have been passed down over generations. Some gave evidence in court, but few perpetrators were charged, and even fewer prosecuted.

The method of working the dinghies is as follows: the white man stands on the after 'thwart with an oar over the stern, and sculls the dingy against the tide; the divers all go down together ... [then] ... swim to the boat and clamber in to it to rest, each man's shells being stowed separately.

Edwin Streeter, a pearler from Cossack, 1886

Left

A group of Torres Strait Islander divers in front of their cutter-rigged lugger, c. 1921. These divers used goggles often crafted out of wood.

Wright Collection, WA Museum MHA 1753/11

Above

Two Aboriginal crew on the Herbert Basedow North West Expedition demonstrate their diving prowess, 1916.

Herbert Basedow Collection, National Museum of Australia

HARD-HAT DIVING

Hard-hat diving or 'dress' diving was introduced to the north-west pearling grounds around 1867. It allowed divers to dive deeper and work longer in the colder water, however visibility was extremely limited by the new hard-hat apparatus. For a while, some boats crammed both swim divers and hard-hat divers aboard.

Despite their profession many hard-hat divers could not swim. Instead they walked along the sea bottom or were sometimes dragged by the movement of the lugger. The suit's air valve could be manipulated by the diver to increase the air inside in order to lift themselves over obstacles and 'fly' over barren areas. Almost all dress divers suffered diver's paralysis (the bends) at some stage. Lacking modern decompression chambers, they had to try to recover before surfacing.

Divers relied on their life-line to communicate with their tender above, through a system of coded tugs. The head diver typically located patches of shell, and then directed the diving tender from underwater. Tenders used compressors (manual, then later engine-powered) to provide air to the divers and it was vital that the air hose was not obstructed, as this could prove fatal.

Japanese divers were reputed to be the best divers, working alongside other indentured Asian and Aboriginal divers. Except for an unsuccessful experiment with British divers in 1913, Europeans rarely undertook hard-hat diving.

I been down to forty fathoms at the Darnley Deeps
Searching for the precious pearlshell.
The pearls to keep.

Seaman Dan, *Forty Fathoms*, Torres Strait musician, 2000

Left

Hand-made diving boots weighed ten kilograms each and featured brass toes, lead soles and heavy leather straps.

Department of Fisheries/
WA Museum MHS 0058/02

Above

Aboriginal hard-hat diver Fred Corpus was considered as good as the Japanese divers. In the 1950s, he worked from Broome and Darwin.

WA Museum MHA 1719/11

Left

Japanese diver wearing VP Heinke dress. The woollen cap often included a tassel used to clear fog from the thick helmet glass.

Courtesy Norman Archive

Below

The weight of the helmet, corselet and back and front weights was in excess of 25 kilograms.

WA Museum MHD 319/103

Opposite

One of Paspaley's hookah divers ready to descend. The new cultured pearl industry still required divers to work from sun up to sun down.

Courtesy Rory McGuiness/ Australian Geographic

HOOKAH DIVING

An entirely new phase of the pearling industry began in 1949 after the Western Australian Government repealed the section of the *Pearling Act 1912* that prohibited the production, sale and possession of cultured pearls. In 1956 a Japanese-American-Australian company began operating a new pearl farm at Kuri Bay.

No longer did divers seek out the largest pearlshell: instead they collected smaller, live shell to be grown to maturity in pearl farms. The shell had to be handled with great care as many specimens died moving from the beds to the farm.

By early 1970s advances in pearl diving technology saw the industry transition from hard-hat divers to modern drift diving. Using neoprene wetsuits and simple 'hookah' regulators divers were more flexible to explore the seabed for pearlshell, resulting in significantly higher collection rates. Hookah diving is still used in pearling today and is regulated within the industry. Like the methods that preceded it, hookah diving is not without risk and unfortunately accidents and fatalities occasionally still occur.

Though methods of finding shell have changed, the fundamentals of pearling have remained the same. The shell must attach itself to the bottom, and finding shell still requires expert skills and an intricate knowledge of the different types of seabeds.

You're out at sea for eight or nine days and you're doing eight or nine dives a day from six in the morning until six at night. Eight drifts a day for forty and fifty minutes and then having a twenty minute surface interval, and then back in the same.

Debra Offer, Hookah diver, 2015

SALTWATER COWBOYS

Armed with at best a basic chart and a compass — and their experience and local knowledge — multicultural crews toiled on the pearling luggers, enduring some of the roughest maritime conditions. For weeks at a time, crews lived aboard small wooden boats which were purpose-built for pearling, but lacked basic amenities. They worked from sun up to sun down in seas with some of the biggest tides in the world. They faced cyclones, tide-rips and unforgiving currents that could suck the lugger of an inexperienced captain into vast, destructive whirlpools. The crew lived 'like family' and even today, former lugger crews reminisce about the days when they were 'saltwater cowboys'.

A lovely flotilla upon an emerald sea ... a pretty sight, those twenty-six vessels in line, drifting across the sea. All under mizzen and jib with their divers down.

Ion Idriess, Australian writer, 1937

Neatly coiled 3/8" air hose was purchased in 8 lengths, and 400 ft. (£60) or more was required. The 18 ounce canvas sleeve covered hose connections at both pump and helmet. Seaming twine secured canvas to hose, and 14 or 16 gauge copper wire was used for tying hose couplings.

Courtesy Norman Archive

Lugger under full sail with clinker dinghy on board.

Bourne Collection, WA Museum MHL 322

Diver warmly clad in heavy woollen Dreadnought drawers and long stockings (*kutsushita*), ready to don the twill diving dress.

Courtesy Norman Archive

Lend me your body tonight my bluewater lady
This salty wind is getting to my bones
These lugger sails are moving too slowly
For this saltwater cowboy sailing home.
This ol' copper hat is aching my shoulders
These lead weight boots don't need any spurs
To ride these waves and bareback mermaids
Ah, this Saltwater Country is my home.

Saltwater Cowboy, lyrics by The Pigram Brothers, 1997

Above

Tender on the verandah holds the diver's lifeline.

WA Museum MHD 319/113

Right

Opening pearlshell on the deck.

Wilkinson Collection, WA Museum MHA 1731/04

LUGGER LIFE

Many writers, photographers and filmmakers were enchanted by the sight of the pearling fleets sailing out on turquoise seas with their multicultural crews. For the crews who lived aboard the luggers for weeks on end, however, the conditions were primitive and space was at a premium. There was no electricity, no refrigeration, no running water and no toilets.

Below leaking decks and the foul stench of drying shell were the sleeping quarters, consisting of small wooden bunks squeezed into cramped bow and aft sections of the boat. Lacking portholes, these areas were dimly lit, poorly ventilated spaces overrun with cockroaches. Up on deck, coiled air hoses, helmets and lifelines left little space for the crew, whose movements were also impeded by the diving suits. Pearl meat hung from the rigging added to the smell.

Cooking was done on deck, using a wood-fired or gas burner in a cut-out kerosene tin or 44-gallon oil drum. The cook had to keep up the supply of hot tea and meals for the crew, even though it was often windy and the decks were constantly wet.

There was a hierarchy that ran from head diver to shell-opener, and each man had his own well-defined duties. The head diver was also the 'skipper', or captain. He chose the pearling grounds, the patch to work on and the direction of each drift. The head diver directed the work from the sea bed through a code of tugs on his lifeline — his life, and the success of the dive, depended upon the alertness and skill of his tender. On board, the crew had to work together, with great trust and understanding, to ensure the divers were able to collect as much shell as possible. It was a highly competitive industry, with bonuses based on the size of the catch. However most of the crew members were indentured workers, and they toiled hard for minimal rewards.

Experienced head divers and their Aboriginal crewmen were able to read the currents and tides, and navigate by the stars in the dark. They understood the weather and knew when to head for safety. Aboriginal crew also supplemented the provisions by hunting fish, dugongs, turtles and turtle eggs.

Left

Dry magnetic compass, Fremantle, 1829.

WA Museum MH03.41

Above

Almost every part of the animal was used: the meat hung to dry; the guts pickled and the precious pearl stored safely.

Bourne Collection,
WA Museum MHL 383

Right

It was a hard working life for the pearling crew, but most loved their work on the sea.

WA Museum MHD 319/111

LUGGER CREW

Lugger crews embodied a colourful mix of cultures, each with its own language, cooking style, customs and religion. Crew members came from places such as Malaysia, China, Timor, the Philippines and Japan.

A typical post-war lugger crew consisted of up to ten men: divers, including the head diver and the No. 2 diver; their replacements and 'try' divers learning the trade; two tenders; an engineer to run the engine and air compressor; a cook; and several shell-openers and cleaners. In the days of the hand-pump more hands were required to man the pump.

The crew worked a very long, hard day. Each man had his assigned task, but in the event of an accident would step in to replace an injured man. As everyone shared the quest for shell, life revolved around the tasks and needs of the divers. The hard work, and the need to live in a confined space for weeks on end, in the face of life-threatening risks, brought the men together. Many describe their fellow crew-members as family, regardless of race, culture or position.

A vessel is more than its ribs and rigging: it is a structure, a set of relationships. Fore, aft, starboard, port — shipwright, skipper, sailors, friends.

Kate Lance, author of *Redbill*, 2004

Left

In later years, few pearling masters (visible in white in this photograph) accompanied their fleets.

E.L. Mitchell, WA Museum MHD 393/048

Above

Lugger decks were often wet and foul-smelling, as the shell was opened and cleaned.

Broome Historical Society and Museum 2009-973

Right

Aboriginal crew shared their daily catch of saltwater tucker including shellfish, turtle, turtle eggs, dugong, crabs and oysters.

Arthur Collett, WA Museum MHD 313/63

LUGGER CREW

HEAD DIVER (CAPTAIN OF LUGGER):

I was head diver. Diving is a very difficult, and a unique job ... so many risks when you are down, plus the responsibility for the rest of the families on board.

Kunihiko Kaino, head diver, 2006

We got 2 types one is half-dress, one is full suit. When the sea is much warmer, we use half-suit and much easier to pick up shell. When you ready to go down, you stand up on the side. When they put the helmet on, I feeling dead or alive? Because I know that it is very dangerous job.

Amat Bin Fadal, head diver, 2006

TENDER:

Out on the ocean we had to learn how to handle the lifeline, the lifeline was like a Morse code.

Paul Phillips, Yawuru tender, 2000

I look after the diver ... because that life, I look after the diver's life ... if not, that diver, he get killed.

Hussein bin Abdul Aziz, tender, 2006

ENGINEER:

Started out as a deckhand and then worked as an engine driver. The engine was 'your own baby'. Had to look after it. Every hundred hours, change the oil, filters. You had to crank the engine but never had any trouble. The engine and the compressor worked together. When the compressor was full the engine would cut, but if the engine stopped the compressor still had air for the diver. No one died when I was there but lots of divers got the bends.

'Ossi', Osman Bin Ibrahim, engineer, 2006

Out at sea, every Sunday is day off. Everybody put their dinghy in the water so we come and see each other. Say, 'Hello, how's things? How many shell you get?'

Kamarudin 'Dino' Bin Lusimoen, engineer, 2015

SHELL-OPENER:

I was the tender and the shell-opener. We would also dry-shell on the reefs. I walked away with a couple of pearls. If I found a pearl, I used to hide them in the folds of my trousers. I would sell it for 60 pounds.

Paul Sampi, Bardi Elder, 2015

Above left

Generations of Aboriginal and Torres Strait Islander people formed the backbone of the pearling industry's labour force.

Fred Gray Collection, courtesy WA Museum MHA 1722/06

Above right

Aboriginal crew weighing and grading their shell, 1917.

William Jackson, North West Scientific Expedition, WA Museum DA9312-035

BUILDING LUGGERS

Pearling luggers were ketch-rigged wooden vessels 13–19 metres in length. They were handcrafted and designed specifically to ride low in the water, drift with the current and be easier for divers, in their cumbersome dress, to climb aboard. Lugger designs varied across the north, in response to the different environments, changing technologies and type of pearlshell fishery.

It took roughly a year to build a lugger, using local craftsmen or Japanese shipwrights, although some pearlers bought their vessels from other seaports. Men such as Jack and Richard Hunter, the Aboriginal sons of beachcomber–pearler Harry Hunter, or Jack Parriman and Charlie D'Antoine, built fleets of luggers and clinker dinghies for the pearling masters in Broome.

Shipwrights often built luggers without detailed plans, instead using experience and the naked eye. Aboriginal workers found the tall cadjebut trees for the ribs. The boat's timbers were steamed to shape in 44-gallon drums joined together and heated on fires.

At the end of each season carpenters and other workers stripped the luggers, sometimes sinking them to kill the cockroaches before caulking and repairing them. Worn-out luggers would miraculously reappear brand-new, supposedly having been 'repaired' — a ploy to bypass rules prohibiting boat-building by indentured foreign labour.

It was a pleasure to watch these men working — always at a trot ... Saws, with a long straight handle which pulled to the operator, and adzes — ordinary ones — but for special work a Japanese one with bentwood handle, which could be used to work a design on a stem head. Caulking mallets and irons — the caulker worked from a springy plank stage to get the correct and even caulk, which would spew out when the timber swelled. The seams were payed with pitch below the waterline and putty above ... Sails were cut and sewn in the loft. Our 'master' — cut all his own canvas — sailmaker and tenders seamed and roped them.

Jack Cryer, fleet manager for AC Gregory & Co, c. 1920

Above

Caulking during restoration of *Trixen*, c. 1986.

Patrick Baker, WA Museum HB Tx/274

Left

Streeter and Male Boatshed, 1972.

WA Museum HB ANC 69

Below

Caulking iron and other irons.

WA Museum MH01.218a, b, c, e

Left

Paying the deck seams with pitch after caulking on *Trixen*.

Patrick Baker, WA Museum HB Tx/279

Far left

Stern of a sawn-frame lugger.

Gary Kerr Collection, WA Museum MHD 331/060

Above

Bob Woods proudly holding the model pearling lugger given to him by Jack Hunter, Bardi Elder and renowned boat builder.

Wood Collection, WA Museum
MHP 0006/20

Left

Model pearling lugger, 1969.

WA Museum, donated by Keith Rundell, MH15.001

Local Broome boat builders at Streeter and Male boatshed, Broome, WA, c. 1972. Left to right: Alphonse Martin, Doug D'Antoine, Vincent Martin, Gregory Martin and Jack Parriman.

WA Museum HB ANC 98

And my dad used to have a team there, men. And they used to look for the bend on the boat for the tree. Bent like a shape like a front of the boat. Big tree like that they used to chop down, and well, in those days, that was the skill of my dad when he used to learn how to build. Go to that shape. Put it in that shape and took it in. After doing that, they came in and started chipping away. Shape it up ... Working on that everyday. They had long, long-handled hatchet.

With the ribs of the boat, they got some guys to weld a forty-four gallon drum, like a big boiler. Put all the timbers in, and boil it up, and once they gave it a few hours, the timber would get nice, very soft. That's how they bend it. When they got them bent, and they started work on the ribs, and the keel that was all hammer and chisel.

Peter Hunter Rooboo, Bardi Elder and boat builder's son, 2015

INDENTURE

By 1870, competition, legislative restrictions, and disease had created a shortage of Aboriginal labour in Western Australia's pearling industry. Pearlers looked to Indonesia for recruits. Within a year, Captain Francis Cadell and Charles Broadhurst had imported 50 workers from the Lesser Sunda Islands. Later, 'Malays' arrived from Kupang, Batavia, Surabaya, Macassar, Singapore, Sulu Islands and the Philippines.

These workers were indentured for a set term of employment at an agreed wage, with a guarantee of repatriation afterwards. However, there was little official monitoring of indentured labour.

When new diving apparatus was introduced, Japanese and Chinese recruits arrived from South-east Asia, seeking work that would enable them to send money back to their families. Many never returned home. Foreigners were not permitted to own luggers, but many did, using white 'dummy' owners on the paperwork.

The cultured pearl industry continued to employ indentured workers until the 1980s.

Below

Indentured crew arrived and departed on steamers from the Broome jetty.

State Library of Western Australia 28085P

Below

Catching the train to town — the first stop was the Customs House where they were assigned to pearling companies and master pearlers.

Bourne Collection, WA Museum MHL 642

Right

Malay crew on their way back to town. The work and conditions were tough but many chose to stay with their new families.

Courtesy Bernadette Haji Amat and Lingiari Foundation

Worked for 4 years — did everything from labourer to a diver. I started seeding pearlshell — I learnt by watching the Japanese and had success. We had a good time. When it was time to leave, I was jumping [ship]. Never go back to Malaysia.

Jumali Bin Abdul Rahman, pearling crew, 2006

LAY UP

We lived by the seasons, the spring tide, the neap tide, the full moon, luggers coming in, the luggers going out. That was when Chinatown came alive.

Pearl Hamaguchi, wife of a pearl diver and pearl farmer, 2000

Aboriginal men loading provisions onto the lugger *Tanami*.

Bourne Collection,
WA Museum MHL 760

As night fell hurricane lamps on decks and cabin tops lit up the scene against the outline of low sand hills and darkness or mangroves. The burning scent of joss sticks, cypress shavings, and coir rope drifted to keep off sandflies. There was music from gramophones and concertinas and singing, tuneful or otherwise — according to alcoholic content.

Jack Cryer, fleet manager for AC Gregory & Co, c. 1920

The small wooden luggers of the early days could not carry all the supplies needed for extended periods at sea. Nor could the crews work in the murky waters stirred up by the strong currents accompanying the high spring tides. So they went ashore to look for water and wood, careen their boats, and barter with Aboriginal groups in the sheltered coastal creeks and bays.

The sight of luggers coming into harbour, and lining the shore at low tide, defined the northern pearling ports. The bustle, sounds and cooking smells of the multicultural foreshore camps made them look more like shanty towns than ports of the British Empire.

The dangerous cyclone season, between December and March, was known as 'lay up'. With the boats safe in port, crews and master pearlers could socialise, spend time with their families, or engage in cultural activities while preparing for the next season. The foreshore camps rang with the sounds of hammers and saws as boat-builders, sail-makers and riggers rebuilt the fleet.

Master pearlers were required to provide accommodation for their indentured workers. So boarding houses and makeshift camps sprang up along the foreshores and in the 'Chinatowns' where Asian people and Aboriginal people mixed.

Left

Broome luggers and pearling camps, 1917.

William Jackson, North West Scientific Expedition, WA Museum DA9312-038

IN THE CREEKS

Lay up camps operated in a barter economy. Coastal Aboriginal groups supplied wood, water and women to the crews who came to the creeks on the spring tides and were paid in tobacco, food, alcohol and gifts. These semi-permanent camps were meeting places and provided alternative sources of rations for the local people.

To avoid the long trek back to port, many pearlers set up permanent lay up camps in coastal bays, such as 'Chinatown' at Cape Bossut, Robison and Norman's camp in Beagle Bay, and Harry Hunter's camp at Boolgin Creek. These became permanent settlements for Aboriginal families. Many of these camps, such as Cygnet Bay, have become sites for cultured pearl farms.

Occasionally, creek-side bartering ended in conflict. Sexual diseases were also easily spread in the wake of these contacts. The authorities became increasingly concerned about the mistreatment of Aboriginal people by pearlers, pastoralists and police. An enquiry, headed by Dr Walter E. Roth, led to passage of the *Aborigines Act 1905*, which sought to control the interactions of Asians with Aboriginal people, especially women. 'Natives' were banned from entering the towns or creeks between sunset and sunrise unless they had gainful employment. Unauthorised cohabitation became a criminal offence and remained so until the 1970s.

Luggers used to come into the creeks once a month for wood and water. All the grandpas used to cut the wood. Have 'im ready. And the women ready ... My grannies used to go for that Malays, because the grandfathers used to let them. That was for tucker ... so they could stay out in those places ... Wasn't wrong.

Edna Hopiga Wabijawa, Karajarri Elder, 1999

At watering points such as this soak at Beadon Creek, near Onslow, luggers would pull in for water and wood. The crew 'traded' with local Aboriginal people, including women, commonly referred to as 'Gins'.

Arthur Collett, WA Museum MHD 313/33

Top: Lugger fleet sailing into Willie Creek, north of Broome, WA, for the lay up.

R.A. Bourue, National Library of Australia 3417765

Above: Captain Francis' pearling schooner *Nellie* at lay up in Barred Creek, WA 1909.

Wilkinson Collection, WA Museum MA 1731/06

A typical pearling shed with the necessary equipment for hard-hat diving — in view are suits, helmets, boots, hoses, compressor and lifelines.

Axel Poignant Collection, National Library of Australia 4404602

Broome's pearling foreshore 1906.

Arthur Searcy Collection, State Library of South Australia, PRG 280/1/14/597

We lived by the moon, the full tide. They mostly came in, in the full moon. That's when the tide was high. They couldn't dive anymore. I mean when the luggers came in, yeah, the town came alive. And all the hustle and bustle, you know, talking across the street and everybody's happy and the single men's camps were all open. And of course there is merriment of drinking and eating, and you know, yeah.

Pearl Hamaguchi, wife of a pearl diver and pearl farmer, 2013

Above

Streets and laneways of 'Japtown' crowded with boarding houses, gambling dens, noodle houses, cafés and hotels.

Courtesy Department of Fisheries/
WA Museum MHP 0026/10

Aborigines Act, 1905, Section 39.

IT is hereby notified that all the lands comprised in the area described below have now been proclaimed to be an area in which it shall be unlawful for Aborigines or Half-castes, not in lawful employment, to be or remain (in lieu of those published in *Government Gazette* of 27th November.

Proclamation of Prohibited Area issued under 1905 Aborigines Act

Right

An Aboriginal Elder in front of the Roebuck Hotel, where under the provisions of the *Aborigines Act 1905* (above right) Aboriginal people were barred from entering, and could only stay in town if they had work.

Bourne Collection,
WA Museum MHL 102

IN TOWN

'Chinatowns' and 'Japtowns' developed in the northern towns where thousands of indentured labourers lived during lay up. Here flourished boarding houses, gambling dens, noodle cafés, laundries, emporiums, general stores and photographic studios. During the tropical wet season, the heat and humidity exacerbated tensions among cultural groups living, gambling and drinking in crowded conditions. Sometimes, as in the race riots of 1907, 1914 and 1920, crews retaliated against perceived or real injustices.

In Broome, authorities strove to maintain racial boundaries. Local families were classified by colour and kept under surveillance. Most institutions were segregated, including hospitals, schools and the Sun Pictures outdoor cinema. State laws prevented Asian and Aboriginal peoples from mixing. Men were fined — and deported — for cohabiting with their Aboriginal wives. *The Commonwealth Immigration Restriction Act 1901* prevented Asian people from marrying or owning businesses.

Despite this, Aboriginal and Asian peoples socialised under the cover of darkness and a vibrant community, with its own music, language and cuisine emerged in Broome.

Lay up was also the social season for the town's white elite, who conducted a gracious, leisurely way of life. They entertained in spacious houses well-suited to the climate, and held amateur concerts, cricket matches, regattas, race meetings, balls and church bazaars.

> ***We weren't allowed to associate with the pearling masters. You're coloured people; you're not allowed to talk to white people, to mix with them, unless you were working for them ... you would get in trouble.***
>
> Lexie Tang Wei (dec), wife of Broome pearl diver, 2006

Mahjong gaming pieces.
Courtesy Maya Shioji

№ 198

THE PEARLING ACT, 1912.

FISHERIES DEPARTMENT, WESTERN AUSTRALIA.

PEARL DEALER'S LICENSE.

Louey Ling Tack ...., is hereby licensed to deal in Pearls during the year ending the 31st day of December, 1919, at his place (or places) of business situated at the business premises of James Fong Carnarvon Street Broome or at any other place which is registered as his place of business.

This license is issued under and subject to "The Pearling Act, 1912."

Dated the 22nd day of September 1919

-£10.

Geo. Moodie
Resident Magistrate.

Place Broome

合共銀	天申 18	青雲 17	茂林 16	必得 15	只得 14	有利 13	光明 12	福孫 11	江祠 10	漢雲 9	坤山 8	正順 7	月寶 6	志高 5	逢春 4	榮生 3	攀桂 2	占魁 1
	THUNDER	SMOKE	HONEY BEE	RAT	MOUTH	OLD MAN	HORSE	DOG	STEAMER	DEADMAN	TIGER	PIG	MOON	STEALING MAN	PADLOCK	HALF DEAD	SHELL	WHALE FISH
	安士 36	吉品 35	元吉 34	青元 33	萬金 32	元貴 31	井利 30	天良 29	日山 28	火官 27	太平 26	九官 25	合海 24	三槐 23	合同 22	上招 21	明珠 20	良玉 19
	OLD WOMAN	NANNY GOAT	BLIND EYE	SPIDER	GOLD MONEY	CRAY FISH	SMALL FISH	FATHER	FOWL	TURTLE	FLAG	CROW	DINER BOAT	MONKEY	PIGEON	KITE	MRS	BUTTER FLY

Above

Chiffa ticket, from a popular Chinese gambling game played during layup.

Courtesy Sarah Yu

Left

Pearl dealers had to be licensed, though many pearls were sold as snide pearls.

Courtesy Doug Fong

In the evening we usually go down to Chinatown for a meal or to the pictures, but what I really liked right opposite Tang Wei's, was a boarding house for Asian men. They had a balcony overlooking Chinatown, and there was gentleman by the name of Sarrip, who used to play the banjo or the ukelele. It was really beautiful.

Philip Dolby, Yawuru Elder, 2006

Above

After World War Two, Chinese divers were in high demand, as the Japanese were banned from working in pearling until the 1950s.

Courtesy Doug Fong

Left

Sam Sue, one of Broome's Chinese pearl dealers, in his store.

Axel Poignant Collection, National Library of Australia 1587442

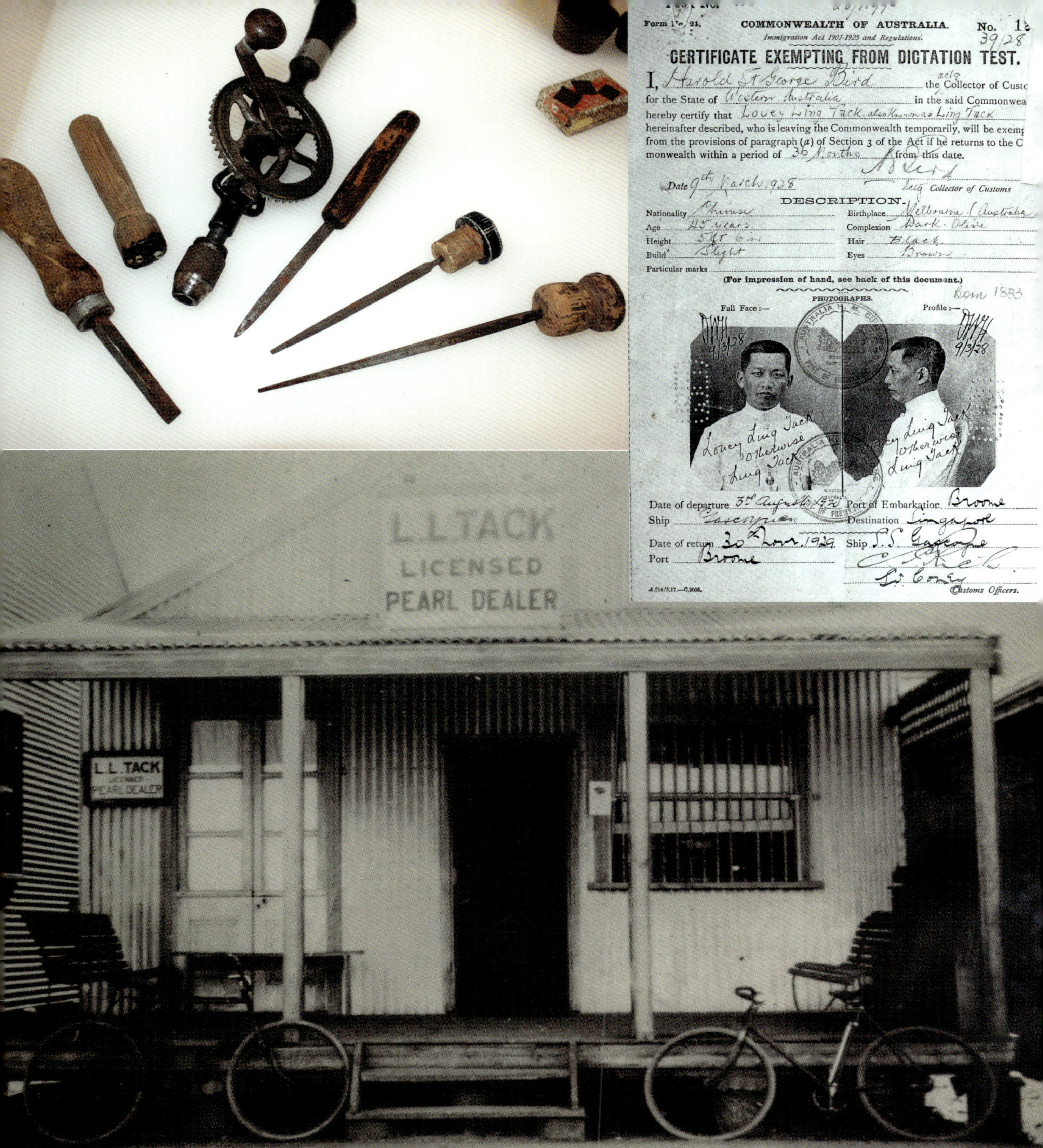

Form No. 21. COMMONWEALTH OF AUSTRALIA. No. 39/28

Immigration Act 1901-1925 and Regulations.

CERTIFICATE EXEMPTING FROM DICTATION TEST.

I, Harold St George Bird actg the Collector of Custc for the State of Western Australia in the said Commonwea hereby certify that Lovey Ling Tack also known as Ling Tack hereinafter described, who is leaving the Commonwealth temporarily, will be exemp from the provisions of paragraph (*a*) of Section 3 of the Act if he returns to the C monwealth within a period of 36 Months from this date.

Date 9th March 1928 — actg *Collector of Customs*

DESCRIPTION.

Nationality	Chinese	Birthplace	Melbourne (Australia
Age	45 years.	Complexion	Dark-Olive
Height	5 ft 6 in	Hair	Black
Build	Slight	Eyes	Brown

Particular marks

(For impression of hand, see back of this document.)

Born 1883

PHOTOGRAPHS.

Full Face :— Profile :—

9/3/28 9/3/28

Lovey Ling Tack otherwise Ling Tack

Date of departure	3rd August 1928	Port of Embarkation	Broome
Ship	Gascoyne	Destination	Singapore
Date of return	30th Nov. 1929	Ship	S.S. Gascoyne
Port	Broome		

Customs Officers.

4.214/3.17.—C.2005.

Top left

Pearl-skinning tools used by Thomas Bastian Ellies in his store at Chinatown, Broome, WA, early 1900s.

Courtesy Peter Ellies

Above

L.L. Tack's former store.

Courtesy Doug Fong

Top right

Papers of indenture, 1928.

Courtesy Doug Fong

Above

Dignitaries including Lord and Lady Gowrie (front row: right and centre) and Captain Goldie (back row, second from right) visiting T.B. Ellies, the pearl dealer store.

Courtesy Aji Ellies (2010)
The Pearls of Broome

Below left

Master pearler H.L. Richardson, pictured, diversified his company by becoming the agent for Siebe Gorman & Co Ltd supplying the fleets with diving gear.

State Library of Western Australia
4323B/69

Below right

Games and events were held during lay up festivities. On the field, cultural differences were overlooked.

State Library of Western Australia
4323B/30

LUGGER PICNICS

At the start of every pearling season, pearling companies and their multi-cultural crews organised festivities, including lugger races, to bless the fleets. Lugger picnics were hosted onboard by the pearling companies for their crews and families. This tradition continued in Broome until the end of the lugger era. Malay and Japanese crew cooked, and on return, festivities continued at the divers' quarters on the foreshore.

It was so exciting ... the lugger picnics ... the whole town went on it, blacks, whites, the whole lot. Food, everything was supplied. We'd go out for a sail and then afterwards we'd have a party at the camp.

Bev Kinney, pearler, 2013

Top right

Muriel in Streeter & Male colours for a lugger race, 1927.

Bourne Collection, WA Museum MHL 229

Right

Chino and Jumahat, Streeter & Male crew, getting ready for the picnic, c. 1966.

Ahmat Bin Fadal, Broome Historical Society and Museum 2009-252

Left

Lugger picnics marked the beginning of the pearling season.

Terence Chenoweth, WA Museum MHD 319/024

MASTER PEARLERS

Master pearler and crew as they haul in their diver. Master pearlers did not usually accompany the crew, but sometimes they joined the fleet mothership.

State Library of Western Australia 4323B/39

They were sea pioneers ... in their fleets of little luggers they charted the entire northern coast from Shark Bay to the Great Barrier Reef.

Ion Idriess, Australian writer, 1937

Master pearlers — or pearling masters, as they called themselves — dominated the social and political life of Australia's north, in towns like Cossack, Broome and Darwin, and as far as the Torres Strait. As powerful colonial entrepreneurs of the pearling industry, they drove the growth and character of these northern centres. However, their strong influence on state and federal governments was disproportionate to their economic productivity.

Above

A lugger fleet laid up on Broome foreshore, 1914. Prior to World War One, pearling was the primary industry of the north-west coast.

State Library of Western Australia 754B/12

WHO WERE THE MASTER PEARLERS?

The popular image of master pearlers is of Anglo-Celtic men in 'pearling whites' and pith helmets overseeing their 'coolie' labour. Yet, in reality, they came from diverse cultural backgrounds, and some were women.

Some early master pearlers were settlers and pastoralists, others were merchant seamen. Many of the early pearlers engaged in slavery and blackbirding to obtain divers and deckhands for their fleets.

Some Asian pearlers owned pearling fleets until they were banned from doing so, others formed 'dummy' partnerships with white pearlers. Some pearlers operated from East Indian ports such as Dobu (Aru Islands) under foreign flags of convenience. They worked outside Australia's three-nautical-mile exclusion zone, evading Australia's fees and regulations.

In the Torres Strait, the London Missionary Society set up Papuan Industries, which allowed communities to build and own luggers to collect shell. Each with its own colours, these 'company boats' were a source of pride and income for the Islander communities.

[A lot of pearlers] served their time in the mercantile marine ... like the old seadogs ... they used to live hard ... most of them have passed on now.

Herbert Kennedy, Broome pearler, 1962

Left

Captain Hilliard with his family and Aboriginal domestic servants, c. 1900s. Hilliard's wife often stayed on her husband's boats, bearing several children at sea. To evade government taxes he operated out of Koepang, Dutch Timor under the Dutch flag.

Jordan Collection, WA Museum
MHP 0058/31

Above

A group of Broome master pearlers in their 'pearling whites'. Most were influential businessmen or held positions of power in local and state government.

State Library of Western Australia
4323B/63

Left

A flurry of activity on Broome's old jetty as master pearlers and their families arrive and depart on the flat-bottomed steamers.

Bourne Collection, WA Museum MHL 463

Below

Inside Hugh Richardson's residence. This photograph depicts a typical master pearler's home.

State Library of Western Australia 4323B/18

Bottom

Yasukichi Murakami on Captain Ancell Gregory's front verandah, 1916.

Courtesy Murakami Family Archives

Bottom left

After her husband died, Mary Dakas entered the male-dominated domain of Australia's pearlshell industry. From 1948, she operated four luggers out of Broome and Port Hedland.

Broome Historical Society and Museum 2006-349d

Above

Stalwarts of the Empire: a group of master pearlers at dinner, with the British flag behind them.

Broome Historical Society and Museum 2006-236

Below

Yasukichi Murakami standing in front of Dampier Hotel, Broome which he purchased with Captain Ancell Gregory so they could attract the best Japanese divers to their fleet.

Courtesy Murakami Family Archives

BLACK BIRDING

From the mid 1800s, coastal Indigenous populations from the Pilbara and West Kimberley were quickly decimated by introduced diseases and exploitation by pearlers. Pearlers ventured further north and inland to remote unregulated areas to procure Aboriginal labour through 'blackbirding' — obtaining workers by deception or force. Such practices were often unofficially sanctioned by authorities, who maintained that the workers volunteered their services. Nevertheless, many missionaries, government officials and ordinary citizens alleged that pearling was based on slavery.

To appease the critics, and the British, who had abolished slavery in 1837, the government drew up pearling regulations in 1871. Fisheries inspectors were appointed to oversee the industry and protect divers, and women were banned from diving.

However, corrupt practices persisted. Aboriginal divers were taken to remote islands, such as the Lacepedes, where fisheries inspectors helped allocate them to pearling luggers. In this highly competitive industry, pearlers such as Charles Broadhurst attempted to use Aboriginal prisoners from Rottnest Island, but, many jumped ship and the venture failed.

Right

Prisoner wrist shackles.

Broome Historical Society and Museum 2007-518

Below

Aboriginal men in chains in Roebourne. Such men were 'blackbirded' by pearlers as labour shortages hampered the industry.

State Library of Western Australia BA1713/2

Left

Glass Kimberley points from Barrow Island, WA. These distinctive glass tools were made by Aboriginal men marooned by blackbirders and pearlers on Barrow Island, 55 kilometres from the Pilbara coast.

Courtesy Professor Alistair Paterson and Professor Peter Veth, Barrow Island Archaeology Project, University of Western Australia.

Left

The 'bare pelt' divers of a pearling lugger at Thursday Island. It was customary to have up to 15 divers on each boat.

State Library of Queensland 45007

MANAGING THE PEARLSHELL FISHERY

Australian pearlers fed the European and American demand for large pearlshell buttons, and for mother of pearl shell, which was used for furniture inlay, musical instrument dials, buckles, combs, cufflinks and the handles of cutlery and revolvers. Until the development of the cultured pearl industry in the 1950s pearls were a lucrative but unreliable side-trade to pearlshell.

The expansion of the north-west was thus driven by pearling. The government was concerned about the sustainability of the industry. Pearlers were stripping pearling beds for short-term gain, a problem exacerbated by the foreign-flagged 'floating stations' beyond government control.

In the early 1870s, in an effort to moderate the industry two key pieces of legislation were passed. *Aborigines, employment in pearling* (*1871*), sought to improve conditions for Aboriginal workers in Western Australia. The *Northern District Special Revenue Act 1873* imposed fees and taxes to fund pearling inspectors. Both Acts were impossible to enforce.

By 1900 pearling was the fourth largest export industry after gold, timber and wool. Western Australia's pearling grounds extended from Shark Bay to King Sound, where jetties, roads, hospitals, stores, jails and courthouses were developed to meet the demands of the pearling fleets.

In 1902 the pearlers formed the Master Pearlers' Association to lobby government. Pearlers also pursued elected office, as members of parliament, councillors and presidents of local councils to ensure they had a voice at all levels of government. Today the pearling industry is regularly reviewed and managed by strict licensing and quota systems.

Master pearler outside the shell shed, with bags of shell ready for grading and packing.

Bourne Collection, WA Museum MHL 582

King Sound was ... the great Eldorado of the Nor-west — the home of the Shells and the Pearls. [Some pearlers] had been successful beyond their most sanguine dreams ... by loading [their] vessels up to the deck beams with shell and making almost a fortune in the one season.

John Brockman, pearler, 1880

Above: Packing shell at the end of Port Hedland jetty, c. 1910.

E.L. Mitchell, WA Museum MHA 1717/09

Below: Broome, c. 1960. For most of the 20th century Broome was considered by many to be the pearling capital of the world.

Reproduced by permission of the Western Australian Land information Authority (Landgate), 2015

BOOM AND BUST: MARKETING PEARLSHELL

Pearling was a lucrative but unpredictable industry, buffeted by forces of over-supply, over-fishing, good and bad seasons, market trends and new technologies. Fleets and crews could be destroyed by cyclones, which could wipe out profits.

Forty years of pearl shelling at Shark Bay denuded the beds, despite belated conservation measures. Intensive shelling stripped the Torres Strait grounds and the pearlers moved to Darwin then Western Australia, but the surplus of shell reduced its value.

After World War One, fashion favoured small buttons, which led to a drop in demand for pearlshell. In response, pearlers fished harder, flooding American and European markets. Japanese pearlers in the Arafura Sea only made things worse by introducing superior diesel-driven 'luggers' with diesel pumps.

Australia's involvement in the Second World War saw pearling suspended. Local Japanese people were interned and pearling luggers were either burnt or requisitioned for the war effort. After the war, a glut of pearlshell and the spread of mass-produced plastic buttons hindered the resurrection of the pearling industry.

The industry was revived in the 1950s with the introduction of cultured pearls, using Japanese investment and technology. Once again, as with pearlshell, Broome produced the world's finest pearls. Since 2008 the world market has been flooded with cheap freshwater pearls, but pearlshell has made a resurgence as a staple of the pearling industry.

The Broome pearling fleet peaked at 403 in 1913, but with the advent of [the First World] War a European economic downturn and a surge in patriotic fever saw the fleet halved as owners and crew rushed to enlist. Many vessels rotted in the mangroves. After the [Second World] War the government wanted to build up the industry again so they made it tax free industry. When they took away the tax benefits in the early 1950s my father's brother abandoned the industry because it was becoming unviable without tax breaks.

Nick Paspaley AO, Pearl Farmer, 2014

Right

Broome pearlers were driven by international demand for pearlshell for the production of buttons.

Beilby Collection, WA Museum MHP 0058/15

The worst blow ... was the 1908 blow. The centre was down at La Grange. We lost 50 luggers and 250 men ... [In Broome] the 1910 blow was easily the worst ... 70 luggers anchored out in the [Gage] Roads and when the blow was over there was one at anchor ... 50 men lost that time.

Herbert Kennedy, Broome pearler, 1962

Above

Pearlers were resourceful and savvy business men and women. Most pearling masters were also pearl dealers, selling pearls and pearlshell as markets ebbed and flowed.

Courtesy Aji Ellies (2010) *The Pearls of Broome*

Below

Devastation on Broome's foreshore after the 1927 cyclone.

Bourne Collection, WA Museum MHL 153

THE PEARLSHELL TROPHY

In 1886 Queen Victoria named a Royal Commission to organise 'an Exhibition of the Products, Manufactures and Resources of the Colonial and Indian Empire'. The Prince of Wales was appointed its president, and he sought to gain 'a more intimate knowledge of the vast fields for enterprise which exist throughout the British Dominions'.

Each colony's 'court', or section, highlighted their region by building trophies, using their produce, to present to the Queen — but also designed to encourage migration to the colony and foster a spirit of enterprise. A pearlshell tower of over 1,000 shells, constructed by the north-west pearlers led by Edwin Streeter, was a highlight of the Western Australian court.

The lustrous pearlshell tower was likened to the column on top of which Syrian fifth-century AD ascetic saint Simeon Stylites lived. However the fate of the tower remains unknown.

> *The crown and glory of the West Australian section [is] the trophy of giant mother-o'-pearl shells, a Simeon Stylites of nacre, glistening and glinting in silvery sheen, no less than one thousand shells being used in its construction.*
>
> *The Inquirer and Commercial News*, 18 August 1886

The pearlshell trophy dominating the Western Australian court at the Colonial and Indian Exhibition, London, 1886.

State Library of Western Australia 1062B/3

PEARL AND HIROSHI HAMAGUCHI

In the 1980s Hiroshi Hamaguchi became the first Japanese person to legally own an Australian pearling business in his own right. In the aftermath of World War Two, he had arrived in Broome as a young experienced seaman from the Wakayama prefecture, to work as an indentured diver for Male & Co. Unimpressed with the terrible conditions of working on cockroach-infested luggers, he was planning to return home, but he met his future wife Pearl, a Broome local of Asian and Aboriginal heritage.

Right: Pearl and Hiroshi Hamaguchi

Courtesy Pearl Hamaguchi

My husband graduated from being a diver, because when he came out from Japan, he went to a maritime college after senior high school, so he had a master's degree. He switched over from being a diver to a ship captain on the pearlshell transport boat. But husband was made redundant, so he decided, 'I'd like to try my hand at my own little pearl farm. Just do it to see if I can.' I thought, 'Oh, my God.' You know, my husband is the first Japanese that they granted a pearling licence to.

So we had four sons working. My role in the family business ... well, I was the accountant, I was the book keeper, I was the pay master, public relations officer, I was the secretary, I was the everything. So I was embarrassed because it was so successful.

Pearl Hamaguchi, wife of a pearl diver and pearl farmer, 2013

Below: Members of the Japanese club of Broome. Most of these people were divers, some were also businessmen and pearlers in their own right, but were unable to officially own a pearling licence.

Ms Michiko Okada, courtesy Taiji Historical Archives

PEARLERS AND WHITE AUSTRALIA

The pearling industry flourished during a time of strong anti-Asian sentiment and the 'White Australia' movement. The *Immigration Restriction Act 1901* introduced a dictation test to exclude 'undesirables' from Australia, but master pearlers obtained exemptions for their Asian workers, many of whom could not speak, read or write English. Asians were permitted to work on the pearling grounds for up to three years, but pearling masters extended this time for their good divers. On shore, workers lived in segregated boarding houses. Any misdemeanor, particularly socialising with Aboriginal people, resulted in deportation.

Crews could take disputes with employers to court, but master pearlers and their associates sat on the bench and justice was often one-sided. Each cultural group appointed a leader with a good command of English to represent its interests and issues and manage cultural affairs.

Open minded pearlers, such as Captain Ancell Gregory, formed discreet partnerships with Asian pearlers. Gregory and Yasukichi Murakami built a large fleet and engaged the best Japanese divers. Gregory shocked Broome society by allowing Murakami to stay in his house.

Miss Universe came to Broome and my boss Sam Male, who was president of the Broome Road Board, asked me to take her out on the lugger. We got on well and she asked me to the ball that night, held in her honour. I accepted and arrived dressed in formal wear, only to be turned away at the door by Mr Archer, another pearler. That was Broome in 1960.

Kunihiko Kaino, Japanese head diver, 2006

Below: Percy's box, Broome, with x-ray of interior mechanism. These lock boxes were used for storing pearls on the luggers while at sea.

Broome Historical Society and Museum 2004-2137

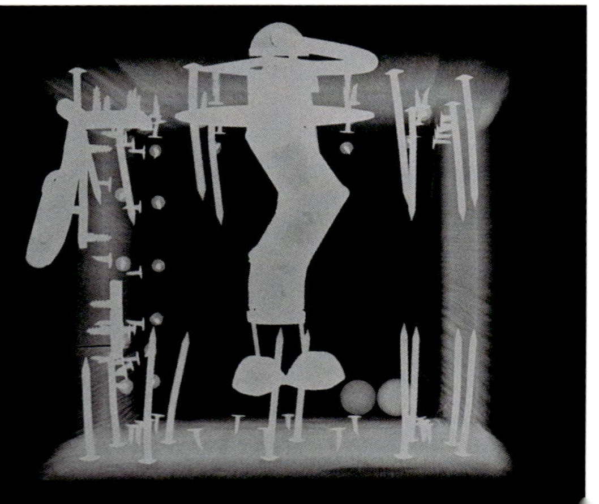

In 1911, Pat Percy, a Broome policeman who became a pearler, patented the 'Safe Keeping Box' commonly known as the 'Percy Box' used to store the natural pearls found in the pearshell. It had a one-way entry point, designed to stop the theft of natural pearls by the lugger crews. The box was brought back to the master pearler for opening. However, this ingenious design did not stop the lucrative trade in snide pearls.

A detailed map on which Ernest Mitchell, Inspector of Aborigines, colour-coded the Aboriginal and Asian populations in Broome.

Note that personal names have been concealed for privacy reasons.

State Records Office of WA, Series 2030, Cons. 993, item 1927/0248

PEARLING ACROSS THE NORTH

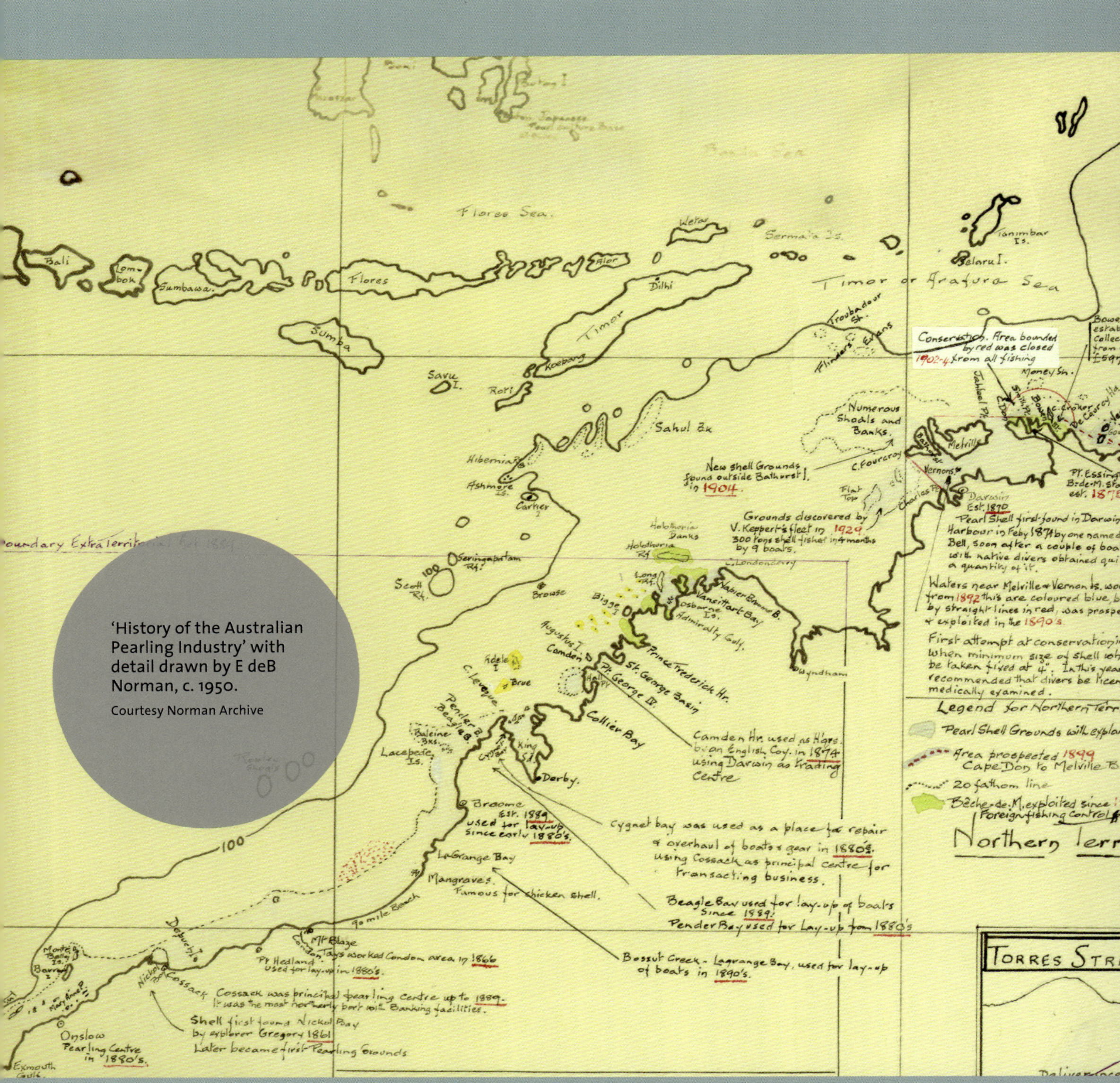

'History of the Australian Pearling Industry' with detail drawn by E deB Norman, c. 1950.

Courtesy Norman Archive

Stretching from Shark Bay to the Torres Strait Islands, the pearling map of Australia is littered with sites and events that populate what was once known as the 'empty north'. Pearlshell beds and 'patches', ancient middens and rock art sites, lay up camps and lonely graves, cyclone paths and shipwrecks, pearling ports and farms create a web of sites that record Australia's pearling heritage.

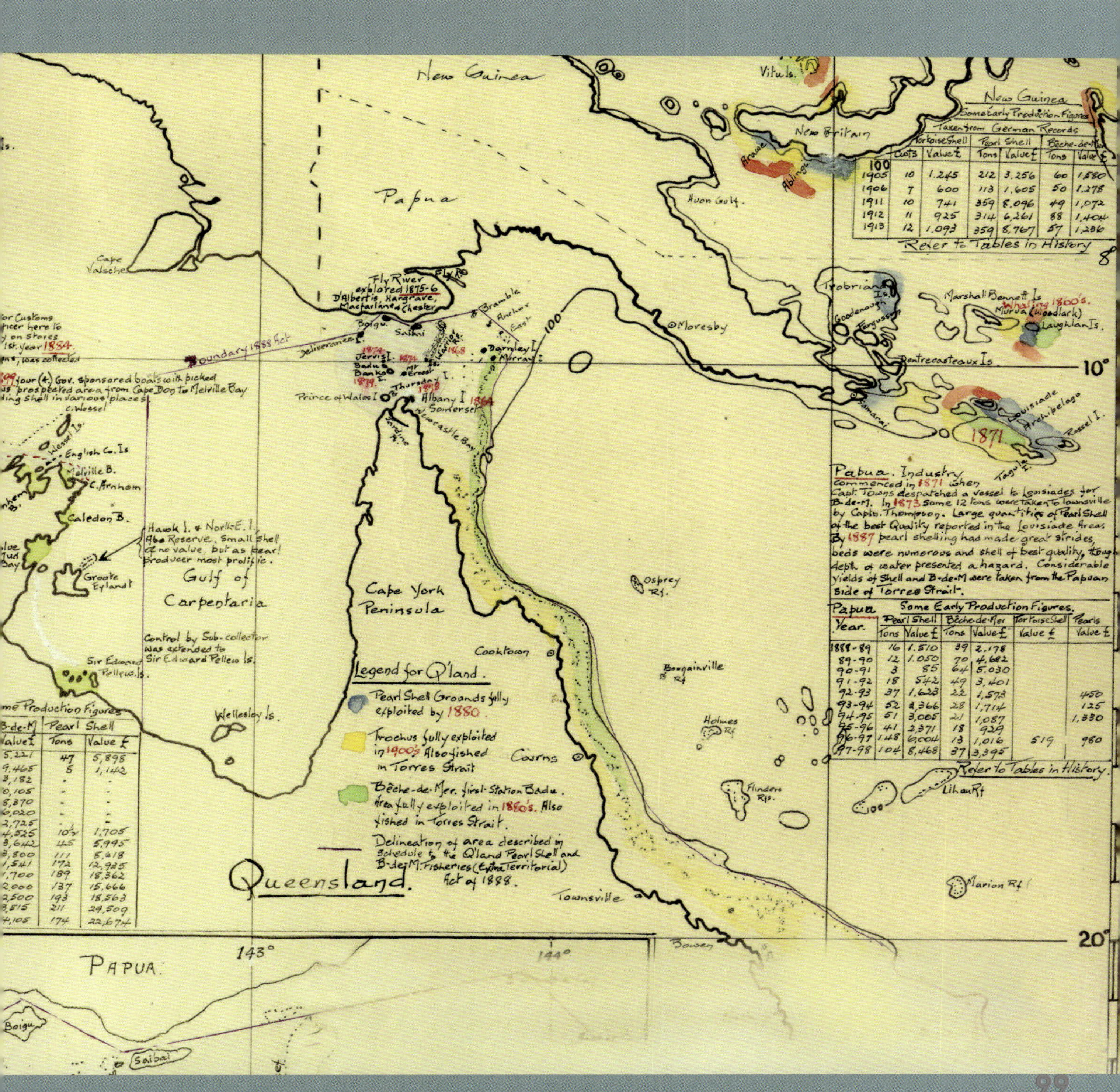

THE LUGGER MEN OF THE CORAL SEA

For centuries, the sea hunters and traders of the Coral Sea and the islands of the Torres Strait shaped and engraved pearlshell (*mai*) into magnificent, masks and body ornaments to celebrate Islander *Zenadh Kes* (cosmology). Trade networks reached the Australian mainland and Papua New Guinea, where pearlshell (*kina*) was highly valued in exchange cycles. The regional historical link to pearlshell remains: Papua New Guinea's major currency is called the kina.

A pearlshell industry developed in the Torres Strait from the 1860s beginning at Tutu (Warrior Island), when European bèche-de-mer fishermen encountered Islanders with pearlshell 'the size of plates'. With their superior seafaring knowledge, Islanders quickly became the backbone of the industry, which eventually attracted a large multi-cultural workforce. As elsewhere in the northern Australian industry, Japanese divers were essential to the Torres Strait industry up until World War Two.

Over the industry's many decades, Islanders worked variously for pearling masters, community-based 'company boats' and family-based sailing dinghy operations. As shallower pearling beds were depleted, divers ventured into ever deeper waters, such as the treacherous Darnley Deeps, which claimed many lives. After World War Two, Islander 'lugger men' traversed the north of Australia working in pearling fleets and later in pearl farms.

Although the industry has waned, the pearling heritage of the Torres Strait is kept alive through stories, songs and art.

Below: By the 1920s, a quarter of the Torres Strait pearling fleet were 'company boats'. Set up initially by missionaries, Islanders were encouraged to buy their own luggers and sell shell to Papuan Industries Limited, a company run by the missionaries and later government officials.

Courtesy Karl Neuenfeldt/Sullivan & Mathams

CYCLONE MAHINA

Pearlers across northern Australia are subject to the mercy of nature. Cyclone *Mahina* struck the Torres Strait region (off northern Queensland) overnight on 4 March 1899. It is widely considered to be one of the most severe cyclones in Australia's history.

The exact measurements and intensity of *Mahina* are not known. Records from a ship which survived the storm indicate the barometer dropped to 880 hectopascals. However, official records reflect a reading of only 914 hectopascals. It is thought the official record was revised to be more believable.

Academics researching *Mahina* suggest only a storm surge of 880 hectopascals could explain the eye-witness accounts. These accounts speak of porpoises being washed onto cliff tops and a police officer washed out to sea from atop a ridge in Bathurst Bay. He spent a week walking back to Cooktown.

Cyclone *Mahina* is often cited as Australia's deadliest natural disaster. Most of the 282 recorded fatalities were due to drowning. The actual death toll is believed to be over 300 people. Records show more than 50 boats were moored in Bathurst Bay at the time the storm hit. Most were pearling fleets working in the area. Captains incorrectly believed the bay would provide shelter from the storm.

The lack of contemporary knowledge about Cyclone *Mahina* is partly attributed to the fact the majority of casualties were non-white. More than twenty countries were represented in the death toll including Japan, Indonesia and Sri Lanka.

Cyclones such as *Mahina* are one of the many dangers faced by pearling crews. Despite technological advancement in mapping of weather patterns, such disasters are still realities for contemporary pearlers.

Well I can remember back from my ... great grandfather, they call Yankee Ned. Well he had two boats. His sons — two was on one boat, and the other two was on the other boat. When that [cyclone] hit Cape Melville, and most of the boats sank, that two survived. They drifted for so long, and by the time the storm died down, they were in the mangroves on the mainland ... They had been away for few months, and [everyone] thought they were dead. But they came back home. All the way from Cape Melville to Yorke Island. They cut mangroves to make new masts and that. They didn't have any compass or whatever, that was in the early days. The reef, they followed the reef. Reefs and I suppose the stars.

George Mosby (great grandson of Yankee Ned), Torres Strait Islander artist and pearler, 2016

TRIBUTE

Once a year, August, full moon time, we go to the cemetery and pray for all our ancestors. We do some ceremony in the traditional way with thousands of lanterns, incense, and Buddhist prayers.

Kunihiko Kaino, Japanese head diver, 2006

The graves in the Japanese cemetery in Broome; most were pearling divers and tenders.

Courtesy Mayu Kanamori

Hard-hat diving is considered one of the world's most dangerous occupations. Before the First World War, at the height of the pearling industry in Broome, up to 30 per cent of the indentured divers lost their lives from disease, cyclones or decompression illness. Official inquiries into the industry between 1912 and 1916 did not adequately address the high mortality rates of pearling workers, and their families were never compensated.

Today, Broome's Chinese and Japanese communities honour those who died with ceremonies such as *Hung Seng* (Feast of the Dead) and *Obon* (celebratory time when the spirits return). There are similar cemeteries in pearling towns across the north of Australia.

Ceremony in the Japanese section of the Broome cemetery, held in front of the obelisk commemorating the 1908 cyclone in which many people lost their lives.

Bourne Collection, WA Museum MHL 198

It was a bad year in 1957. We lost three or four divers. The news came that the B6 was coming in with the flag at half mast. The bush wireless. There were two wives whose husbands were on the boat. We all waited, wondering who will be the widow.

Pearl Hamaguchi, wife of pearl diver and pearl farmer, 2012

GROWING PEARLS

The pearl is the only gem that is made by a living creature ... it represents life.

Marilynne Paspaley AM, Director Paspaley Pearls, 2015

Over millennia people have valued pearls as symbols of prosperity, power and beauty. The development of cultured pearls renewed the pearl's significance.

Courtesy Cygnet Bay Pearls

Only about 20 per cent of cultured pearls are spherical.
Courtesy Paspaley Pearling Company

Pearls are rarities of nature — aquatic gems produced through a biological process rather than a geophysical process like diamonds and other precious gems.

Attempts to harness the natural beauty of pearls and pearlshell have been documented since the time of Ancient Greece.

In the second century AD, the Greek writer Philostratus described in *Life of Apollonius* how divers would pierce pearls with a long pin in order to extract a white liquid which they collected in small iron moulds. In thirteenth-century China, carved pieces of wood and lead were inserted into mussel shells to create nacre-covered figures of Buddha.

Though people have tried to grow them for thousands of years, spherical pearls were not successfully cultivated until the early twentieth century, on Japanese Akoya pearl farms.

Later, the technique spread to Australia and across the world. As the pearlshell market slowly declined, determined Australian pearlers forged a new era, producing cultivated pearls for high-fashion jewellery.

UNLOCKING THE CULTURED PEARL

Round pearls are cultivated by implanting a nucleus in an oyster. The oyster secretes layers of nacre around it, forming a pearl. This intricate technique, called 'seeding', took centuries to perfect.

The first European to grow pearls was probably Swedish naturalist Carl Linnaeus, who inserted limestone beads into mussel shells in 1761, producing small but poor-quality pearls. Other Europeans followed with similar results. In Australia in the late 1800s, naturalist William Saville-Kent experimented with techniques similar to those used in thirteenth-century China. By inserting hemispherical beads into oyster shells, he successfully produced mabe or half-pearls.

A breakthrough occurred in 1904, when two Japanese scientists, Tatsuhei Mise and Tokichi Nishikawa, patented a technique to cultivate round pearls. They may have benefited from the work of Saville-Kent, who discovered the technique but died before he could publish it.

Japanese pearler Kokichi Mikimoto introduced cultured round pearls to the global market in 1916, but Japanese technicians guarded the technique, and it was decades before Australian pearlers joined the new market.

Above

Saville-Kent's photograph of an 'experimental pearl-shell cultivation site' in Broome, WA, c. 1897. His experiments were driven by concerns about the sustainability of natural pearl beds.

Courtesy William Saville-Kent (1897) *The Naturalist in Australia*

Above

Cultivated half-pearls, also known as mabe or blister pearls.

Courtesy Cygnet Bay Pearls

AUSTRALIA'S NEW PEARLERS

Early experiments in growing pearls were banned in Australia because of lobbying from the pearlshell industry, who feared competition. In 1921 Australian pearler Ancell Gregory, working with Japanese entrepreneur Yasukichi Murakami, attempted to establish a cultured pearl farm in the Montebello Islands (130 kilometres off the Pilbara coast).

However, the farm was prohibited after other pearlers lobbied against its potential threats to the pearlshell market. The next year, the Western Australian government passed legislation banning the manufacture or trading of cultured pearls. By mid-century, though, Australia's traditional pearling industry was barely alive: men and luggers were lost to war, and plastic buttons were destroying demand for pearlshell. In 1949 the ban was repealed.

Australia's first cultured pearl farm, Pearls Proprietary Limited (PPL), opened at Kuri Bay in 1956. Japanese pearlers provided technical skills but guarded their pearl-culturing knowledge closely. Finally, in the 1960s, after tireless experiments, Lyndon Brown from Cygnet Bay Pearls, was the first non-Japanese technician to cultivate round pearls. Brown shared his methods with Aboriginal colleagues Aubrey Tigan Galiwa, Tom Wiggan and Gordon Dixon.

In the next decades, farms proliferated along the north-west coast, including Cygnet Bay, Morgan, Paspaley, Kailis, Blue Seas, Arrow, Cossack, Maxima, Dampier, Clipper, Norwest and Hamaguchi — Australia's first Japanese-Aboriginal owned pearl farm. By the 1990s, the industry was booming.

A gem-quality pearl is so rare and difficult to produce ... all our pearls tell the story of a century of human risk and endeavour.

Penny Arrow, Pearl Farmer, 2007

The rafts at Kuri Bay.

Courtesy Mario Marlos

Early pearl seeding raft at Cygnet Bay, first entirely Australian-owned pearl farm.

Courtesy Cygnet Bay Pearls

Kuri Bay in the 1960s. The farm was named after company principal Tokuichi Kuribayashi, of Nippo Pearls.

Courtesy Trevor Gorey

THE EVOLUTION OF PEARL FARMING

Australia's pearl farmers worked hard in the quest to grow perfect pearls. They devoted themselves to the care and wellbeing of oysters to maximise pearl growth and quality while facing continuous challenges of cyclones, predators and issues around oyster health. PPL and Paspaley pioneered a transition from rafts to submerged longline systems which spread shells further apart beneath open water, and anchored them on lines to guard against currents and monsoons. This was later refined by Arrow and Dampier to enable pearl farming in rough open water sites, while Kailis and others introduced a raft of new techniques and standards of pearlshell husbandry.

To grow pearls, companies began collecting young shells instead of large, mature ones. These had to be transported rapidly to the pearl farms, prompting Cygnet Bay to introduce the industry's first modern fibreglass pearling vessel. In 1974 Paspaley unveiled the *Paspaley Pearl*, the first 'floating laboratory'. This signalled the end of luggers — technicians could now clean and operate on oysters in-situ, before transfer to the farms.

Pearlers continue adapting to this day, with innovations such as hatchery-bred shell, which bolster farms' wild stocks. However, they still contend with major environmental threats like cyclones and the effects of climate change on shell health.

The quicker you can do the operation, the better. Each oyster I operated on reacted differently. Some will be very tense. Some will be relaxed and I would have to adjust myself to the oyster how they would take me touching it. Obviously because something foreign is about to come into their body so they try to close up, and then you have some that don't mind it.

Jasmyn Cook, pearl seeder for Arrow Pearls, 2015

Left: Pearl technicians develop intimate connections with the live creatures they operate on — the success of a pearl farm is literally in their hands.

Courtesy Jasmyn Cook

Far left: Pea crabs live inside every healthy oyster, technicians have recognised they may help an oyster's hygiene and wellbeing.

Courtesy Jasmyn Cook

[You have] to understand the environment to a whole new level so you can not only keep this animal alive but make it thrive and keep it safe ... whilst it slowly grows a precious gem in it.

James Brown, Pearl Farmer and Marine Biologist, 2015

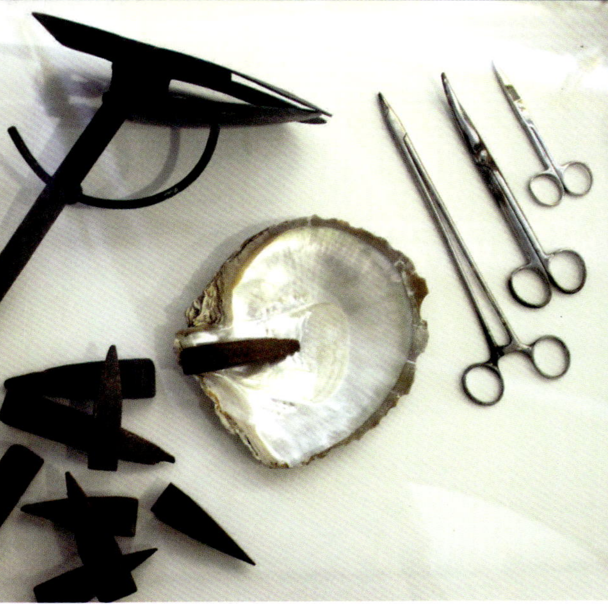

Above top and opposite

The longline system gives shells more space than the raft system introduced by Japanese pearlers at Kuri Bay.

Courtesy Cygnet Bay Pearls

Above

Tools used for seeding and harvesting pearls.

Wooden wedges, from the Estate of Denis George, Australian National Maritime Museum 00044074; Pearlshell holder, donated by Steve Arrow, WA Museum MHO10.223a; Operating tools, courtesy Cygnet Bay Pearls

Above top

A rare Australian 'keshi' strand featuring 23 seedless pearls measuring 21.10mm x 13.20mm, assembled by Bruce and Alison Brown after decades of collecting unusually large keshi pearls from each harvest at Cygnet Bay pearl farm.

Courtesy Cygnet Bay Pearls

Above

Cygnet Bay's Lyndon Brown with mabe pearls. These pearls were easier to grow, providing cash flow while pearlers refined techniques to cultivate round pearls.

Courtesy Cygnet Bay Pearls

SELLING PEARLS

Natural pearls are rare and highly valued, with exceptional ones attracting big prices. Through economic tides they have maintained a market: from Cleopatra's fabled priceless pearl to the Peregrina pearl, prized for nearly 500 years and sold in 2011 for over £7 million ($13.7 million). Australia's 'Southern Cross Pearl' was said to be worth £10,000 ($19,500) in 1886.

Streeter and Male were among the first to deal in pearls in Western Australia, during the late nineteenth century. In Broome, the industry was booming and they were joined by Chinese dealers like Sam Sue and Louey Ling Tack. Jeweller and trader Thomas Bastion Ellies from Ceylon (now Sri Lanka), was known for his proficiency at 'skinning' pearls (surgically peeling away imperfections). Outside the legal trade were 'snide' pearls, smuggled from luggers, usually by shell-openers.

A pearl's value is determined by five virtues: its lustre, shape, size, surface quality (skin) and colour. However, as with all gems, beauty and rarity also add value.

Above

Natural pearls from Thursday Island in 1921. They range in size and shape, from perfectly round to irregular baroque.

National Library of Australia 3314159

Above

Pearl dealer Sam Sue at his Broome shop on Sheba Lane, the 'street of pearls'.

Stuart Gore, State Library of Western Australia 022181PD

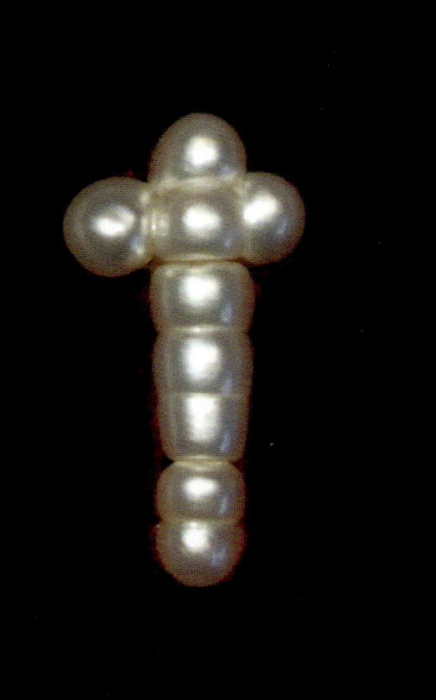

The Southern Cross Pearl was found by locals, Shiner Kelly, Jim Clarke and Clarke's son, Tommy, while diving for crayfish and pearl shells off Baldwin Creek, near Broome, in 1883. The shell was highly unusual, consisting of a natural baroque (unevenly shaped) pearl cluster roughly in the shape of a cross. In 1886 it was exhibited as part of the pearling centre-piece of the Western Australian Court at the Colonial and Indian Exhibition in London and attracted great interest. The last survivor of the syndicate owning the shell was Charles Peto-Bennet who took possession of it around 1914.

After its last public showing at the 1924 British Empire Exhibition, the Southern Cross Pearl disappeared from public view. After much searching and intrigue, it finally surfaced again in 1981 at Christie's in London.

Top

Southern cross pearl.

On loan from Chris Peto-Bennet L2006.1 WA Museum

Above

The array of colours of Australian South Sea pearls from the *Pinctada maxima* pearlshell.

Courtesy Cygnet Bay Pearls

THE NEW MARKET

The emergence of cultured pearl farms in Australia transformed the pearl market as an entirely new product — the largest and finest quality cultured pearls the world had ever seen — quickly caught the attention of international buyers.

As Japanese cartels controlled the market until the 1990s and Japan was the global centre of pearl trade, most pearls from Australia were presumed to be a 'product of Japan'. Today, with dominant sellers like Paspaley and Autore Pearls, buyers have come to recognise that the largest and rarest 'South Sea Pearls' are in fact, a product of Australia.

Despite their successes, Australian pearlers face serious economic instability. The industry was severely hit by the 2007 global financial crisis and is still recovering, with only a small number of producers and sellers operating today. They face growing competition from Asian hatchery-bred oysters and freshwater pearls. Pearlers have responded to this by promoting the beauty of Australia's pearls, the remarkable history behind their production, the untouched wilderness environments in which the *Pinctada maxima* is sustainably collected and grown, and the presentation of bespoke Australian South Sea pearl jewellery for future generations to behold.

Below

Shimmer Vibrance earrings.

Courtesy Kailis Australian Pearls

Below

Jewellers working at Paspaley's Jewellery Atelier.

Courtesy Paspaley Pearling Company

Above

Australian South Sea pearls are some of the largest and most lustrous in the world.

Courtesy Paspaley Pearling Company

What is the perfect pearl? A pearl is graded and valued on lustre, size, shape, colour and the skin ... But ... beauty is in the eye of the beholder.

Patricia Kailis AM OBE, Governing Director MG Kailis Group, 2003

CONTINUING TRADITIONS

Aubrey Tigan Galiwa (dec) applying red ochre to his pearlshell design.

Patrick Baker, WA Museum
DSC7119

I am one of the riji (pearlshell) carvers. That's my life. My grandfather and father taught me the old designs. That's how I tell the story of my country and the history of my people. I pass this on to my young people to take over from me.

Aubrey Tigan Galiwa, Mayala Elder (dec), 2012

Below

'Storms' by Garry Sibosado, Lombadina, West Kimberley, 2014.

From left to right: *Riidalb* (north) *Janjal* (east), *Badbagoon* (south) and *Goolarli* (west).

Courtesy Garry Sibosado

The Australian pearling industry has survived by adapting to new conditions, embracing tourism and exploring new markets for pearls and shell.

Today, in the face of change and concerns about the preservation, relevance and vibrancy of pearling's history, Aboriginal Elders, current pearl farmers and old pearling families all share a desire to preserve, retell and reaffirm their pearling heritage.

In this way, we the Yawuru people, hope that the stories of harvest and many uses of pearlshell will remain strong.

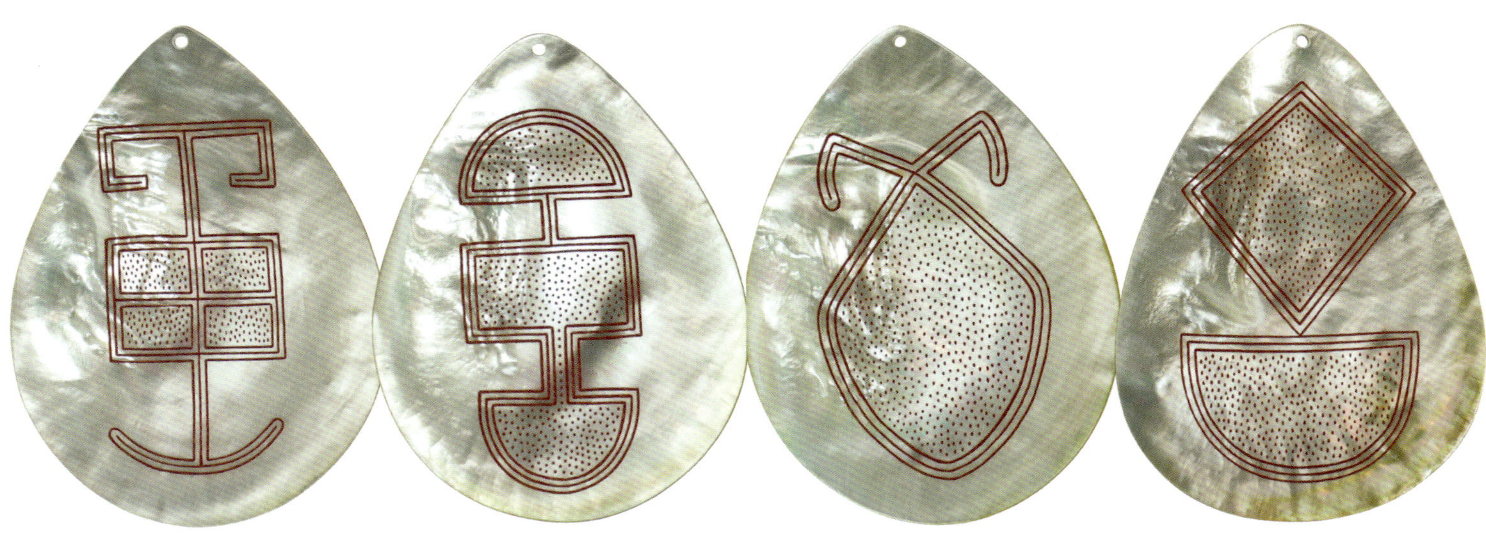

To me pearlshell carving is all about the culture, being proud of who I am, of keeping our culture going. It's about keeping the story alive.

Russell 'Wossy' Davey Jooda, Bardi pearlshell carver, 2015

Above left

Russell 'Wossy' Davey Jooda with the shell he carved for the Bardi dancers.

Courtesy Sarah Yu

Above

Trevor Sibosado carving pearlshell.

Moya Smith, WA Museum MS 1988-07-33

Opposite

Aubrey Tigan Galiwa (dec) demonstrating pearlshell engraving to his grandson Lennox Tigan.

Courtesy Sarah Yu

OUR PEARLING HERITAGE

Aboriginal Elders maintain their ancient knowledge of pearling, passing on traditions of harvesting, decorating and using pearlshell to younger men.

Master carvers and Elders such as Aubrey Tigan Galiwa, Sandy Paddy Malilboor and Roy Wiggan Bagayi were determined to pass on their *riji* carving skills and designs to the next generation. Paying homage to their teachers and the past, younger artists carve traditional designs and create new ones. Contemporary carvers including Wossy Davey, the Sibosado brothers, Sebastian Arrow and Bruce Wiggan continue to engrave the country and its spirit onto shell.

Over the past 100 years, carved shell for wider markets, including pearlers, missionaries, tourists and collectors, has become an additional element in the artistic suite. Highlighted with natural ochres, many *riji* carved by Kimberley coastal artists present realistic drawings that tell the story of country and of historical experiences. These and traditional *riji* are now found in ethnographic and art collections around the world.

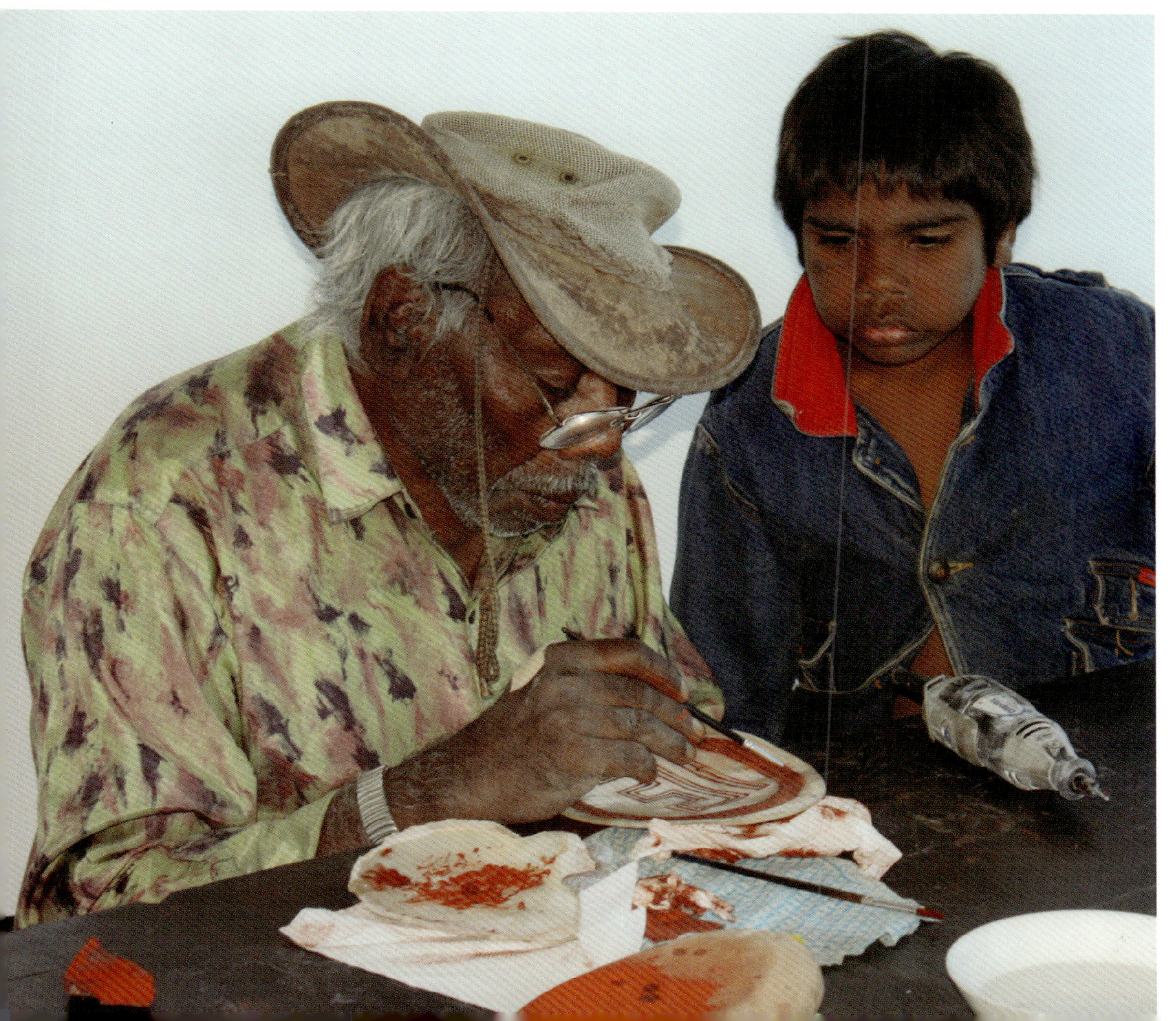

CONTRIBUTING TO SCIENCE

Nacre, or mother of pearl, is widely prized for its qualities of lustre, lightness, strength and porosity. But in the modern world pearlshell has inspired many other innovative uses in fields as diverse as human health and environmental controls.

Recent research into the structure and physical properties of mother of pearl has generated a model for developing mechanisms of bio-mineralisation. These can be used in bone regeneration or to harden the glass used in mobile devices, such as phones and tablets.

The capacity of the large *Pinctada* bivalves, or pearl oysters, to process large volumes of water and remove large quantities of suspended particulate matter enables them to act as biomonitors for their own environment. The wide global distribution of pearl oyster species also makes them suitable candidates for monitoring programs of marine pollution, both regionally and globally.

Even the humble clothes button has now become a focus of historical–archaeological research. Archaeologists such as Celeste Jordan have developed new isotopic and trace element analytical techniques to study mother of pearl buttons in order to identify the source of the shell and the age of the buttons. This will help to date archaeological sites where buttons have been found, and enable the global distribution of Australian pearlshell to be tracked.

The next generation of artificial bone may rely on a few secrets from the sea ... We allow nature to guide the process [of making artificial bone]. Seawater can freeze like a layered material, so why not use this property to cast ceramics that mimic nacre ... We are half a micron away from mimicking nature.

Prof. Antoni Tomsia, Berkeley Labs Materials Sciences Division, 2015

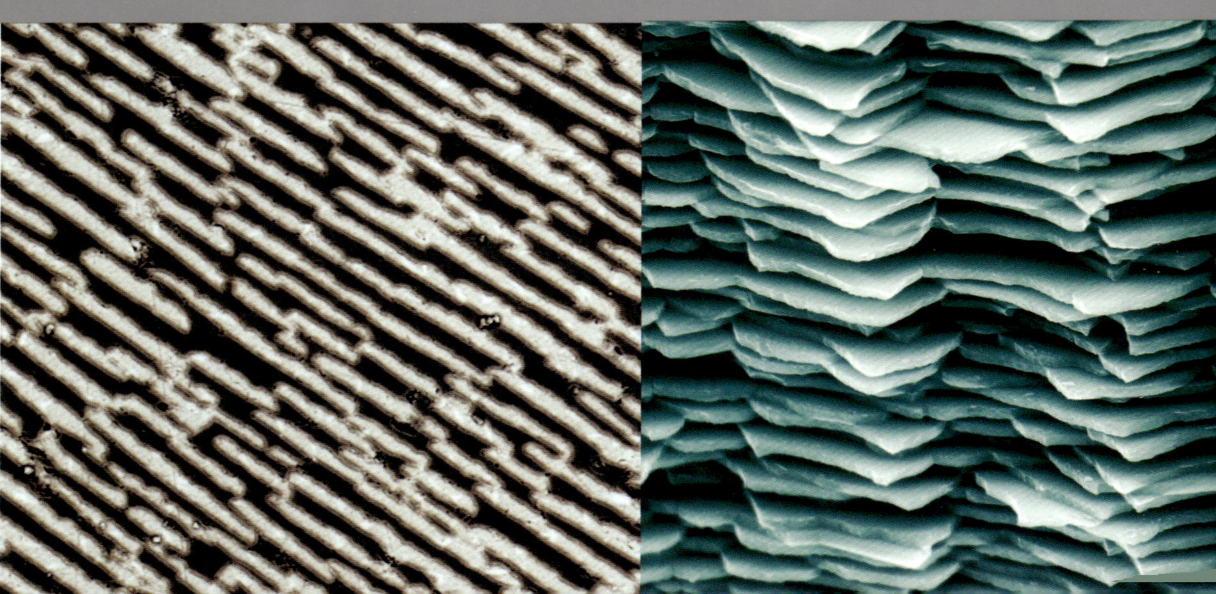

This metal-ceramic composite (left) developed by the Berkeley Lab team resembles the microstructure of nacre (right).

Courtesy Prof. Antoni Tomsia, Berkeley Lab's Materials Sciences Division

LOOKING AFTER PEARLSHELL COUNTRY

In the past, pearlers sometimes exploited shell beds recklessly. Over time, however, practices have improved and pearling is now an environmentally benign industry. Nevertheless, pearling faces new threats.

A mysterious disease, not yet fully understood, is killing adult shell. Climate change is affecting coastal waters. Other industries threaten the pristine marine environment where pearlshell lives; oil spills impair water quality, mooring chains scrape the bottom of the seabed and increasing marine traffic disturbs the waters.

The pearlshell beds of Eighty Mile Beach are some of the best in the world, and they continue to be central to the lives of the Indigenous people who live there.

As younger artists continue to engrave pearlshell, rangers and cultural workers are looking after pearlshell beds as a way of honouring Saltwater Country.

Like the 'Warriors of Roebuck Bay' whom Saville-Kent photographed in the 1880s, these young Yawuru men stand on the middens of Kennedy Hill, Roebuck Bay, where the Yawuru have recently declared a marine park. They work as rangers, curators and tour guides and are committed to the preservation of the bay and protecting the pearlshell beds of the north-west Kimberley coast.

Below left to right: Bart Pigram, Luke Puertollano and Dean Mathews.

Courtesy Damian Kelly

Australia's pearlshell beds are managed with environmental sensitivity ... Australians have forgotten, or maybe never knew, the importance of pearling. Oil and gas mining walk straight over it ... and it's nothing short of a tragedy.

Nicholas Paspaley AO, Pearl Farmer, 2014

Cygnet Bay is not just a farm. It is a community. It's a family home. When I reflect on our journey it is really a story of relationships and the way people work together to get through what would now be considered incredibly difficult and challenging ordeals.

James Brown, Pearl Farmer and Marine Biologist, 2015

Above

Marking the end of the pearling lugger and hard-hat diving era in the late 1980s, *Kunmunya* departs Streeter's Jetty bound for the pearl farm at Kuri Bay. *Lugger B5*, also known as *DMcD*, lies in the creek that was the site of the first landing of the pearlers of Roebuck Bay. *DMcD* has since been restored and now stands in Broome's Pearl Luggers Museum.

Courtesy Maria Mann

Left

The close working relationship between Aboriginal families and the Brown family continues today at Cygnet Bay.

Courtesy Cygnet Bay Pearls

The last veterans of the hard-hat industry are passing away, and the pearling beds are under new threats. The challenge is to remember, understand and appreciate the multicultural history of Broome and the northern coast of Australia.

We need to look beyond the idea that pearlshell and pearls are mere trophies to be acquired and sold. We need to perceive the intricate web of connectedness that exists between the shell, its habitat and the people who harvest it. Most of all, we need to recognise our responsibility to look after it.

We hope that this salute to our pearling traditions will inspire you as we find ways to protect Australia's rich pearling heritage. It is an unbroken story that spans more than 20, 000 years.

galiya mabu

Goodbye and thank you

The pristine waters of Cygnet Bay with *Ardinagoon* (Shenton Bluff) above.

Courtesy Cygnet Bay Pearls

I am Yawuru and also of Jabirrjabirr descent, and grew up in Broome. Our old people along the north-west coast used guwan (pearlshell) long before the arrival of European settlers and have continued their traditions to this day.

Since the pearlers came there has always been someone from my family working in the industry, including myself. We discovered that my great, great, great grandfather William Bryan was a blackbirder who took a Jabirrjabirr woman and had a child, who is my ancestor in the Dampier Peninsula. He was eventually charged in Roebourne for the abuse of native crewmen by tying them to the mast of the schooner Annie Taylor in 1889.

This is my heritage and part of Australia's pearling story. It is etched in the land and we should know and respect these stories, the people and where they came from.

Bart Pigram, Emerging Curator, Nyamba Buru Yawuru, 2015

Emerging curators Bart Pigram and Maya Shioji with Nyamba Buru Yawuru guest curator Sarah Yu, at the exhibition launch of *Lustre: Pearling and Australia* at the Western Australian Maritime Museum, 2015.

Courtesy Sarah Yu

Last year my dad passed away. He was one of Broome's last hard-hat divers. Working on Lustre with aunty Sarah, Bart and the amazing team from the WA Museum was an opportunity to connect with my father's life story and to appreciate all the hardships he went through. It was also an opportunity to celebrate the rich multi-cultural heritage of Broome.

Being an emerging curator on this exhibition was a once-in-a-lifetime opportunity and I was proud to be able to tell the Indigenous story of pearling which is close to my heart and my family.

We are all proud of being able to bring together people who share a passion for pearlshell country, and to help keep the art of pearlshell carving alive.

Maya Shioji, Emerging Curator, Nyamba Buru Yawuru, 2017

ACKNOWLEDGEMENTS

We acknowledge the late Aubrey Tigan Galiwa for his inspiration, commitment and generosity in sharing his story and art for this exhibition. We thank the Yawuru, Karajarri, Bardi, Jawi, Mayala Elders (past and present) and their organisations for their guidance, support and contributions. Finally, thanks go to the Wunambal, Gaambera, Gooninyandi and Torres Strait Islander people and the local people, storytellers and musicians of Broome and beyond for their support and contribution.

We also acknowledge and thank the individuals and institutions who loaned objects and images for inclusion in this publication and in the various iterations of the *Lustre: Pearling and Australia* exhibition. Without your support this exhibition would not have achieved the success it has and this publication would not have been possible.

CONTRIBUTORS AND LENDERS

Kim Akerman, Patrick Amadieu, Christian Amadieu, Penny Arrow, Steve Arrow, Dr Jane Balme, Ahmat Bin Fadal, Helena Bogucki, Annie Boyd, Jacqui Brisbout, James Brown, Lyndon Brown, Robyn Caddy, Joseph Christensen, Jasmyn Cook, Russell 'Wossy' Davey, Martin Dexter, Senator Patrick Dodson, Hugh Edwards, Aji Ellies, Peter Ellies,Sharon Ellies, Doug Fong, Dr Stephen Gapps, Trevor Gorey, Bernadette Haji Amat, Pearl Hamaguchi, Honourable Dr Kim Hames MLA, Damien Hassan, Dr Patricia Kailis AM OBE, Anna Kaino, Kunihiko Kaino, Mayu Kanamori, Damian Kelly, Gwen Knox, Michel Lawrence, Pat Lowe, Maria Mann, Mario Marlos, Rory McGuiness, Ewen McPhee, Dr Karl Neuenfeldt, Professor John E de Burgh Norman, Debra Offer, Michiko Okada, Marilynne Paspaley AM, Nicholas Paspaley AO, Dr Alistair Paterson, Chris Peto-Bennet, Mrs Rosalind-Ruth Phelps, Carl Phillips, Bart Pigram, Dr Roslyn Poignant, Dr June Ross, Jordan Shields, Maya Shioji, Garry Sibosado, Fiona Skyring, Melissa Skyring, Dr Katherine Szabo, Tigan Family, Professor Antoni Tomsia, Michael Torres Jalaru, Eric Van Ees Beeck, Dr Peter Veth, Ken Walton, John Wilson, Sarah Yu.

Arrow Pearls, Australian Geographic Magazine, Australian National Maritime Museum, Bardi Dancers, Broome Historical Society and Museum, Buru Energy Ltd, Cygnet Bay Pearls, Department of Fisheries, Derby Wharfinger Museum, Form Gallery, Goolarri Media Enterprises Pty Ltd, Honolulu Museum of Art, Horniman Museum and Gardens London, Kailis Australian Pearls, Kimberley Aboriginal Law and Culture Centre, Landgate, Lingiari Foundation, Macleay Museum at the University of Sydney, Materials Sciences Division at the Lawrence Berkeley National Laboratory, Mimbi Community, Murakami Family Archives, Musée de la Nacre et de la Tabletterie, National Archives Australia, National Gallery Australia, National Gallery of Victoria, National Library of Australia, National Museum of Australia, Norman Archive, Nyamba Buru Yawuru, Paspaley Pearling Company, Short St Gallery, South Australian Museum, State Library of Queensland, State Library of South Australia, State Library of Western Australia, State Records Office of Western Australia, Subiaco Antiques, Sullivan and Mathams, Taiji Historical Archives, University of New England, University of Western Australia, University of Wollongong.

QUOTES

Unless specified below, quotes were sourced from Nyamba Buru Yawuru or Western Australian Museum oral histories and interviews collected for ***Lustre: Pearling and Australia.***

p. 29 Dr Lindsay Joll, 1991
Doubilet (1991)

p. 40 The Pigram Brothers (1997)
The Pigram Brothers attribute this line from Saltwater Cowboys to Micky Mathews (dec), Yawuru musician and ex-pearling worker, 1981

p. 44 Jimmy Poland, 2012
FORM Gallery (2013)

p. 49 Edwin Streeter, 1886
Streeter (1886)

p. 50 Seaman Dan, 2000
Seaman Dan (2000)

p. 54 Ion Idriess, 1937
Idriess (1937)

p. 56 Pigram Brothers, 1997
The Pigram Brothers (1997)

p. 60 Kate Lance, 2004
Lance (2004)

p. 62 Kunihiko Kaino, 2006; Paul Phillips, 2000;
Hussein bin Abdul Aziz, 2006; 'Ossi' Osman Bin Ibrahim, 2006
Goolarri Media Enterprises (2008)

p. 62 Amat Bin Fadal, 2006
Goolarri Media Enterprises (2006)

p. 65 Jack Cryer, c. 1920
Kerr (1985)

p. 69 Jumali Bin Abdul Rahaman, 2006
Goolarri Media Enterprises (2008)

p. 71 Jack Cryer, c. 1920
Kerr (1985)

p. 82 Ion Idriess, 1937
Idriess (1937)

p. 85 Herbert Kennedy, 1962
Charlton (1962)

p. 91 John Brockman, 1881
Brockman (1912)

p. 93 Herbert Kennedy, 1962
Charlton (1962)

p. 94 Inquirer and Commercial News, 1886
'Western Australia at the Exhibition' 1886 p. 1.

p. 101 George Mosby, 2016
Mosby (2016)

p. 115 Patricia Kailis, 2003
Kailis (2003)

REFERENCE MATERIAL

Akerman, K., and Stanton, J., 1994, *Riji and Jakoli: Kimberley pearl shell in Aboriginal Australia*, Northern Territory Museum, Darwin, Northern Territory.

Brockman, J., 2010, *Pearling Days*, ed. PJ Bridge, Hesperian Press, Perth, Western Australia.

Charlton, M., 1962, 'Four Corners in Broome in 1962', *Four Corners*, television programme, Australian Broadcasting Commission.

Doubilet, D., 1991, 'Australia's Magnificent Pearls', *Australian Geographic*, vol. 80, no. 6, pp. 109–111.

Edwards, H., *Shark Bay through four centuries 1616 to 2000*, Shark Bay Shire, Shark Bay, Western Australia.

Ellies, A., 2010, *The Pearls of Broome*, CopyRight Publishing, Brisbane, Queensland.

FORM Gallery, 2013, *Pieces of Gutharraguda (Shark Bay) Jimmy Poland: Jewellery and Objects*, catalogue, 6 September to 11 October 2013, FORM Gallery Perth.

Goolarri Media Enterprises, 2006, *Old Broome: Five Great Stories That Bring Broome's History To Life*, DVD, Goolarri Media Enterprises, Broome, Western Australia.

Goolarri Media Enterprises, 2008, *Return of the Pearling Legends*, DVD, Goolarri Media Enterprises, Broome, Western Australia.

Idriess, I., 1937, *Forty Fathoms Deep*, Angus and Robinson, Sydney, New South Wales.

Kailis, P., 2003, 'The Passion for the Perfect Pearl address to the WA Business News Success and Leadership Series', transcript, 11 June 2003.

Kerr, G., 1985, *Craft and Craftsmen of Australian Fishing 1870–1970: An Illustrated Oral History*, Mains'l Books, Portland, Victoria.

Lance, K., 2004, *Redbill: From Pearls to Peace: The Life and Times of a Remarkable Lugger*, Fremantle Arts Centre Press, North Fremantle, Western Australia.

Mosby, G., 2016, *Interview with Donna Carstens at Canopy Arts Centre, Cairns, Queensland*, transcript, 9 June 2016.

Norman, J.E. deB. and Norman, G.V., 2007, *A Pearling Master's Journey: In the Wake of the Schooner Mist*, Strathfield, New South Wales.

Saville-Kent, W., 1897, *The Naturalist in Australia*, Cambridge University Press, Cambridge, UK.

Seaman D., 2000, *Forty Fathoms*, MGM Distribution, Sydney, New South Wales.

Strack, E., 2006, *Pearls*, Rühle-Diebener-Verlag, Stuttgart, Germany.

Streeter E.W., 1886, *Pearls and Pearling Life.* George Bell & Sons, London, UK.

The Pigram Brothers, 1997, *Saltwater Cowboy*, MGM Distribution, Sydney, New South Wales.

'Western Australia at the Exhibition', *The Inquirer and Commercial News (Supplement)*, 18 August 1886, p. 1.

Yu, S., and Brisbout, J,. 2011, 'In Mayala country with Aubrey Tigan for the Indigenous Heritage Project', report, Department of Environment, Heritage, Water and the Arts, Canberra.

SPONSORS

Robyn Caddy — Founding member of The Victorian Button Collectors Club Inc.

CONTRIBUTING AUTHORS

Robyn Caddy
Anneliese Carson
Tanya Edwards
Michael Gregg
Lisa Kirkendale
Bart Pigram
Maya Shioji
Isabel Smith
Moya Smith
Polly Smith
Corioli Souter
Sarah Yu

Published 2018 by the Western Australian Museum
49 Kew Street, Welshpool, Western Australia 6106
(Postal: Locked Bag 49, Welshpool DC, WA 6986)

www.museum.wa.gov.au

Reprinted 2021.

Designed by Johanna Standish-Hansen.

Printed in China by Everbest Printing Company.
ISBN 978-1-925040-33-3

Inside cover image:

Riji (engraved pearlshell) by Aubrey Tigan Galiwa (dec), depicting the pearlshell beds or 'patches' of the Lacepede Islands.

Courtesy Aubrey Tigan Galiwa, Mayala Elder

Cover image:

Thistle under sail, passing another lugger.

WA Museum MHD 319/114